Believe it
Think it
Achieve it!

A practical guide to analyzing your beliefs and managing your thoughts to create the life that you truly desire.

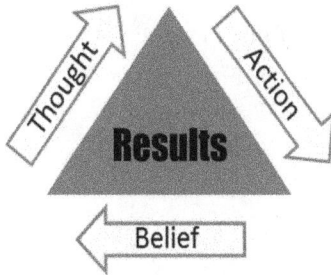

© Institute of Intentional Belief

Sidney McCartney

Library of Congress Cataloging-in-Publication Data

Published by The Institute of Intentional Belief
www.intentionalbelief.com

ISBN-10: 0-9886962-0-7
ISBN-13: 978-0-9886962-0-4

Printed in the United States of America

CONTENTS

SECTION I – Belief

SECTION II - *Thoughts*

SECTION III - Actions

SPECIAL NOTE

I am extremely grateful to have been chosen to share this information that has been a burden on my heart. With much love and thankfulness, I beseech the Creator of all life for guidance and prosperity in my own life and the life of others.

I, in and of myself, know nothing in the grand scheme of things. I am but a speck when compared to the universe, but the words that I have been chosen to deliver are larger than a thousand universes. The power that is within me is far greater than I. But through a divine connection with this eternal power, I am able to tap into the deepest realms of reality to reveal that which has already been revealed to me.

So many times I have been emotionally moved by the words that have flowed effortlessly out of my mouth and from the tips of my fingers. I am in awe at the premise and concise messages intertwined within each sentence that I have written. The life lessons included within have been amassed after years of pain and suffering and are meant to enlighten those who seek to find purpose and fulfillment in life. Indeed, these messages have transformed my life; my desire is that it will do the same for you!

"The hardest part is believing in the face of adversity... everything else is easy"

- Sidney McCartney

DEDICATION

The contents of this book have been amassed consciously and subconsciously over time due to the encouragement and love of two special women in my life:

Rachael Edwards and Pauline McCartney; my grandmother and mother respectively.

I dedicate this book to them for all of their passionate and caring efforts and their belief in me when I myself did not believe.

I love you both!

SPECIAL THANKS

Warm heartfelt thanks go to Alison Yager, who shared this incredibly enlightening journey with me.

"Belief in oneself must not come with resistance from within"

- Sidney McCartney

"In order to reach a goal, you must believe 110%, 110% of the time"

- Sidney McCartney

HOW TO USE THIS BOOK

Believe It, *Think It*, **Achieve It**! is intended to be read and reread as many times as needed in order for the principles contained herein to be absorbed into your conscious and subconscious mind. Your current system of beliefs has not been built overnight, but has been built "brick" by "brick" over an extended period of time. Therefore, dismantling this system of beliefs and reconstructing a new system of beliefs is a continual process. Each piece of "brick" that fabricates your current system of beliefs must be dismantled and new "bricks" must be laid in its place.

The rate at which this occurs is not predicated upon some magical formula, but is determined by your level of desire and commitment to change your life. The process may take hours, days, months or even years; all depending on your level of desire. It is far too easy to forget the principles contained herein and revert to the old ways of thinking. For this reason, it is highly recommend that this book be read and reread to continue to enable and empower you in this reconstruction process. The chapters are designed to be read daily. It is recommended that you read them *before* you go to bed so that your subconscious mind has the opportunity to absorb the information without being distracted by the hustle and bustle of life.

Simply reading Believe It, *Think It*, **Achieve It**! once, may instill certain principles but, remember that your current system of beliefs may be deeply rooted in your subconscious mind and thus will require additional work on your part. However, do not become discouraged if you are not able to initially grasp the concepts. Simply continue to read the passage and return to it at a later time. This will enable you to avoid the frustration of attempting to completely absorb the new material the first time around.

Each chapter is divided into four main sections:

- ¤ Idiom or chapter heading.
- ¤ Main body that explains the chapter heading.
- ¤ Questions related to the chapter heading.
- ¤ Additional space for notes or revelations.

The main lesson and premise of the chapter is presented in the chapter heading, which is further explained in the main body of the chapter. At the end of each chapter, there are a series of questions related to the premise contained in the chapter. The purpose of each question is to incite the production of another question that will help you to gain clarity through self-analysis. Feel free to make notes in the section provided; actually I highly encourage it. It will allow you to become highly interactive with the contents of this book and your life. The caveat here is that these questions must be answered in all honesty so that you can reap the full benefit of the chapter. After each question is answered, indicate the date on the line provided. This date will serve as a reference point to indicate what your beliefs and thoughts were as of that date and how they have changed after re-reading the chapter at a later date.

It is my desire that you thoroughly enjoy every portion of this book and benefit tremendously from an infusion of mindfulness. Remember, be patient as you seek to evoke a change in your life. It will be worth the effort!

"Therefore I tell you, whatever you ask for in prayer, <u>BELIEVE</u> that you have already received it, and it will be yours"
- Mark 11:24

PREFACE

B elieve It, *Think It*, **Achieve It**! rose from the ashes of my utter despair, frustration and fear. For years, I agonized over the lack of desired success and fulfillment in my life; however, my desires seemingly continued to be illusive. My spirit began to be "shaken" as I bore the brunt of a seemingly endless barrage of assaults that I had surreptitiously created. However, in my darkest hour, a ray of hope glimmered through the rising smoke that was my life.

My quest for answers led me on an intense three year journey of epic proportions. This expedition encapsulated a continuous study to identify patterns in my life as well as the lives of others and eventually produced a climactic enlightenment that embodied my involvement in the curriculum of the school of disbelief. Malevolently, I had been counteracting my every movement towards success and fulfillment through my lack of belief in the possibility of success and fulfillment.

Believe It, *Think It*, **Achieve It**! incorporates a fundamental mixture of science, spirituality and philosophy that can be used to reposition your life. It incorporates a system which enables you to gain an understanding of your own beliefs and perceptions by providing you with a framework for analyzing and managing these beliefs. The messages contained within are inspirational in nature; the sole purpose of which are to aid you in the construction of an awareness of the process of mindfulness and self-analysis with the intention of identifying how you are actively influencing and creating the results in your life.

Believe It, *Think It*, **Achieve It**! approaches the realm of positive thinking not from the exclusivity of "positive thinking" or "affirmations", but rather addresses the source and not merely the symptom. Unlike typical books that advocate "positive thinking" as a daily diet, Believe It, *Think It*, **Achieve It**! is a revelation of how merely focusing on positive thinking without first addressing the underlying limiting beliefs is simply not enough to effectively produce the desired changes in your life. Believe It, *Think It*, **Achieve It**! uses practical examples to highlight how the process of "positive thinking" is merely an attempt to obtain your desires without addressing the underlying destructive beliefs that are driving your thoughts.

Remember, you do have control over the experiences in your life through the definition of creating your desires in life through the power of your beliefs. You no longer have to live your life as though it is being viewed through a foggy window. Now as your life unfolds based on your specifications, you can step from behind this foggy window to joyously participate in the life which you have created.

BEL I EVE

Look closely at the word "believe". Without the letter I, the word "believe" would simply not be the same. It is positioned harmoniously within the center of the word, balanced on both sides by three letters. The very essence of this word is captivated by the letter "I", thus it is not possible to remove it. Symbolically, each of us is represented by the letter "I", since belief must originate from within each of us. In order to ignite the possibilities of belief, you must call upon the "I" in believe and continually state, "I believe"…"I believe"…"I believe".

Belief is personal yet definitive to each individual because it literally defines the individual. Belief is a statement of functional operation in the mind that is held to contain some level of truth. All of your subsequent thoughts and actions are based on this statement of operation as it relates to the creation of "reality" in your mind. However, in order to function optimally, you must possess a fundamental understanding of what constitutes "your reality" and how this "reality" affects your interaction with the "world" within and around you.

Your "reality" is based on the degree of awareness and mindfulness to which you choose to perceive the world within and around you. However, please note that there are major differences and implications between awareness and mindfulness. They are both different but completely interrelated and can be categorized relative to the impact they have within and without.

WITHOUT:

Mindfulness, as a precursor to awareness, can be defined as a process of continually monitoring your beliefs, thoughts and actions, knowing that it is through the correct mix of all three that outward awareness is heightened and allowed to flow into your life. The answers to all of your questions are readily available however, it is an incorrect mixture of belief, thought and action that dilutes the ability to perceive or become aware of what already exists. For example, fear inherently limits your ability to perceive and become aware of solutions that are obvious and evident.

WITHIN:

Mindfulness becomes a subset of awareness in that although mindfulness highlights the awareness of how your beliefs, thoughts and actions affect the outcome of your life however, without an awareness of opportunities beyond your conceptualized belief system, your mindfulness will only encompass a limited view of the available options. There must be a desire to move beyond your current comfort zone in order to increase your current level of awareness. This desire will bridge the gap between what defines your current perception and other available perceptions.

Belief, thought and action is a triad system that forms three points of connection. They are not only interrelated but also interdependent. One element of the triad cannot be altered without creating a positive or negative affect on the entire triad system. Since belief is the foundation that formulates our reality, it promotes specific thoughts and actions based on this belief, which in turn creates results in our lives that reinforce the original belief. However, a decision to alter one's beliefs will result in a production of different thoughts and actions, cumulatively resulting in a different result.

Traditional belief is belief that is filled with limitations whereas intentional belief is limitless. Traditional belief is actually belief intertwined with disbelief. These limiting beliefs are so easy to proliferate because we have been conditioned through the school of disbelief. For example, "You can achieve anything you set your mind to" is a common empowering mantra however, "What makes you think that you can do that?" is another common mantra that is counteractive to the first. Unfortunately, these disempowering mantras are much more prevalent than their positive counterparts. Therefore, it is no surprise that believing and thinking in the positive have become such a chore for most of us.

All of our beliefs and thoughts have an origin. The compilation of our past experiences is used to produce the beliefs, thoughts and perceptions of our present and future experiences. However, much of this information is so deeply buried within our subconscious that we may not be aware of its existence. Unfortunately, the scars from past experiences can discolor our present and future beliefs and perceptions. It may be bewildering for us to realize that many of the seemingly subtle and forgotten experiences have shaped us into the person we are today. However, most of us only have an affinity with the experiences we can consciously recall while subsequently disregarding the ones we are not "able" to immediately recall. Even though these experiences may be stored tightly away in our sub-consciousness, they do have a strong determining impact on our lives.

We are the author of our beliefs and thoughts. This principle empowers us with the ability to alter them at will. However, this process will be met with a bit of resistance from our old mode of thinking that has become a seemingly permanent fixture in our minds. But these beliefs and thoughts are by no means immutable unless we decide to make them absolute. Notably, our past experiences have trained us to think in a certain way; we think like our friends, family or peers because we have become domesticated to thinking in this way. But just like our other habits that can be changed, so too can our current habitual thinking be changed, provided we have the right amount of determination and commitment.

Determination can be defined as an absolute resolve to achieve one's desires however, in order for this determination to function as intended, one must be committed. Commitment without passion is commitment that is not passionate. However, the level of commitment is based on the passion for that which we choose to believe. Passion affects our beliefs because it affects our commitment to this belief. Therefore, we must not only believe in whatever we desire to accomplish in our lives, but our desires must be filled with absolute passion for what we desire. This passion will serve as the driving force that will keep us fixated on our belief with anticipation. Remember, determining one's passion requires self-analysis not only of what is believed as possible, but also of what is believed as impossible based on our current set of limiting beliefs. (Refer to Appendix IV).

Unfortunately, most of us do not mindfully engage in the process of self-analysis in order to define how our limiting beliefs are actually functioning as predetermined assumptions. We simply make these assumptions based on a chosen lack of awareness and then we react to these assumptions. Predetermined assumptions are limiting in that they encapsulate our beliefs and thoughts to an awareness that is only based on the limitations of the assumption. For example, a lack of finding a solution to our current situation is actually a lack of awareness of a solution that already exists.

Belief is literally a dichotomy with vastly different potential outcomes. Belief knows no race, gender or other characteristics that we typically use as definitions. It can function as a double edged sword in that it can create positive elements while simultaneously creating negative elements in our lives.

The process of intentionally altering our current beliefs and thought patterns is one that involves intentionally and purposely replacing our outmoded disempowering beliefs and thoughts with empowering beliefs and thoughts while believing and focusing intently on these positive replacements. Whenever we possess disempowering beliefs and thoughts, we must immediately dispute their validity and subsequently replace them with beliefs and thoughts that are constructive.

For example, thoughts of non-deserving have no basis because no matter which negative experiences we had in the past, we do deserve a life of abundance and fulfillment.

We have the power to intentionally choose our thoughts...

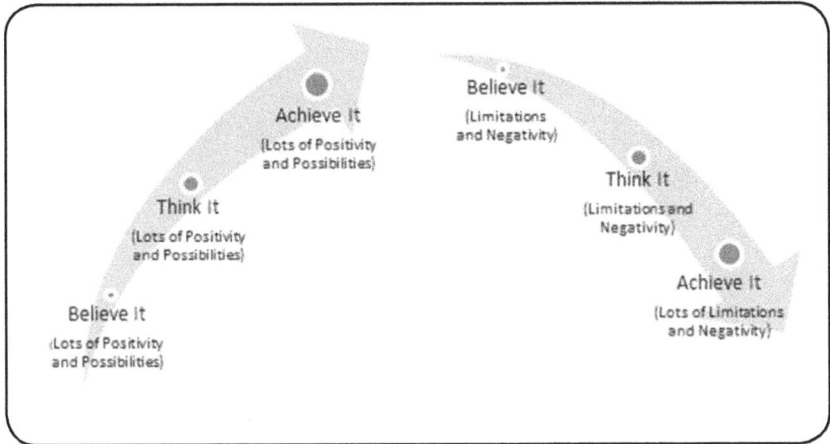

Achieve It
(Lots of Positivity and Possibilities)

Believe It
(Limitations and Negativity)

Think It
(Lots of Positivity and Possibilities)

Think It
(Limitations and Negativity)

Believe It
(Lots of Positivity and Possibilities)

Achieve It
(Lots of Limitations and Negativity)

Replace these disempowering thoughts of non-deserving with empowering thoughts of deserving. Repeat this process as often as needed until they become habitual. However, we must be patient! This process of deliberately and intentionally replacing the disempowering beliefs and thoughts with empowering counterparts will eventually become habitual in nature, causing the disempowering to eventually give way to the empowering. But the process must be performed consistently, since it was through a consistently habitual process that the original disempowering beliefs and thoughts were initially fostered. Anytime we allow even an ounce of negativity to rest in our minds, we are risking a loss in momentum and therefore a loss in our ability to achieve our goals. However, through the process of mindfulness and an appetite to achieve our desires, our awareness will be heightened, thus making way for a life filled with rich new experiences.

Belief

YOU DO NOT HAVE TO BELIEVE EVERYTHING YOU BELIEVE

What a novel idea! You do not have to believe everything you believe. But what do you believe if you do not believe what is emanating from your mind? Well let's examine the process of believing. The origin of our beliefs stems from our earliest experiences. Unfortunately, most of these experiences result prior to our understanding of the power of belief and the application of mindfulness. As children, we were typically told that we can accomplish anything we put our minds to, but our experiences with others and our surroundings often contradicted this statement. Our friends, family and peers were always busy "trying to make ends meet" as they focused on expense reduction and the safety inherent in following the masses. Therefore, our lives were often filled with the essence of sacrificing in order to get ahead. It is no wonder that many of us developed beliefs based on limitation and poverty consciousness. Nothing worthwhile can be attained without lots of hard work and sacrifice seemed to be the common mantra. In Principle, we have been conditioned under the school of limiting beliefs.

This is by no means an attempt to destroy the good intentions of our parents, but if their lives also lacked complete fulfillment, they too have been conditioned under the school of limiting beliefs. They were probably under the false assumption that life must be lived in a prescribe manner commensurate to the masses. However, the prescribed manner to which they were referring is based on the prescribed manner of limitations. A child raised in a wealthy environment will not typically possess the stigmatism associated with money and sacrificing as does a child raised in poverty and rightfully so. Belief of what was possible was instilled by their friends, family and peers and was accentuated by the presence of wealth in their lives, making it far easier to perceive greater possibilities than their counterparts.

Even though our parents had noble intentions, these intentions were based on a theory of limitation and thus produced a false positive in our lives. Consequently, we eventually believed that we had to sacrifice in order to obtain our desires; our accomplishments must be within a particular threshold based on the masses and nothing worthwhile in life comes easily. Thinking outside the box of convention was a direct violation of the social norms! However, a desire to achieve more out of life presents an opportunity to become aware of the limiting beliefs that have been engrained in our mind from our earliest recollections.

Our new found awareness will create a challenge to all of our preconceived notions. Contrary to popular belief we do not have to sacrifice our physical and emotional well-being in order to obtain what we desire! When our focus is on sacrifice, our focus is literally on the lack of ability to produce abundance in the present or in the future. Ironically, we have been conditioned to believe that our source of abundance is only relegated to a limited number of sources. We are not living in a world that is based on a foundation of lack. If one source of abundance is depleted, another is always available.

Our ability to accomplish is not mandated by the masses, but is mandated by what we choose to believe. If we accept the threshold imposed by the masses, their threshold becomes our threshold, even if our original perception was of an even greater threshold. Expand more.

To think outside of the box of convention is to think in a way that is in direct contradiction to the school of limitation.

This box figuratively confines you mentally and therefore physically. But who created the box in which you appear to be confined? Did you place yourself in this prefabricated box? By accepting the predeterminations of others, did you take it upon yourself to construct your own personal box of limitations?

As a child, I can recall having visions of manufacturing space craft to explore the outer reaches of space. But anytime I would convey this desire to friends, family and peers, I received blank stares that bordered absurdity. Why would it be deemed impossible for a kid living in the Bahamas, with no telephone, unpaved roads and the proliferating evidence of sacrifice all around him, to conceive of constructing space craft some day? Within my mind, the notion was absolutely possible because I created a vision of this success in my mind. However, the preconceived limitations of others offered no compelling encouragement on its possibility of attainment. I did however have the love and support of my mother and grandmother, without whom I probably would not have maintained the motivation to continue my passionate drive towards success.

Even though your life is an embodiment of your beliefs, you are free to choose to alter this embodiment. An awareness of the past limitations coupled with an appreciation of your current awareness must necessitate a deviation from the old limiting beliefs that plague your life. You do not have to believe everything you believe since what you currently believe may be based on a foundation of limitation and false positives. But what you MUST believe however, is in your ability to look beyond the accepted limitations and create whatever life you can envision in your mind regardless of the perceived limitations that surround you.

Are you under the impression that what you currently believe is absolute?

How would your life evolve if you embraced a higher belief?

Notes:

Date:_____

YOU ARE THE GREATEST THING TO HAPPEN TO YOU

M any of us do not understand nor appreciate the great power potential we possess when it comes to our ability to dictate the direction of our lives. Often, this immense power potential is taken for granted as we scurry from day to day, attempting to accomplish the numerous tasks in our lives. But we have much more power and control over our lives than we realize. This power is activated by what we believe, think and perceive; the results of which ultimately depend on what we decide to do with them.

The ability to choose our destiny separates us from the animals. An animal cannot decide to become a doctor or an astronaut, however, we can. We can invent; we can create and we can decide the direction of our lives. We have the ability to analyze our beliefs, thoughts, emotions and actions to determine how they are actually contributing to the negativity in our lives. This is the power that we all possess!

Unfortunately, this power is seldom used, due to a lack of awareness that any amount of negativity in our lives will cause the creation of further negativity and doubt in our minds. This doubt will dispel the notion that not only is our desires possible, but they are also personally achievable. The presence of any type of disbelief will affect the power potential of our desires and ultimately the results of our lives.

Our limiting beliefs were originally created and accepted by us. However, we have the power within us to produce a change through the identification and corrective alteration of these limiting core beliefs by:

◆ Identifying our core limiting beliefs

Our core beliefs are the backbone for the types of thoughts we have on a daily basis. Therefore, we can identify the associated limiting core beliefs through the identification and examination of our disempowering thoughts.

◆ Elimination of core limiting beliefs

Self-limiting core beliefs naturally produce thoughts that are limiting. These destructive beliefs are designed by us and as such are not immutable. They can only survive if we give life to them through our continued focus. We can, in so much as we have created these destructive beliefs, decide to create new constructive beliefs based on a determination in our ultimate success. Our limiting thoughts will be eliminated through the elimination of the negative beliefs identified in the previous step. Through constant emersion, we will eventually render these new thought patterns habitual.

All of your choices, thoughts and actions originate from the beliefs in YOUR mind. Even though things around you may appear as though they are not going according to your desires, you can still control the ultimate outcome. You are the greatest thing to happen to you in the sense that you and only you have the ability to control the ultimate direction of your life. You may be affected by external forces, but the final decision is ultimately up to you. You can decide if your life will head in a positive direction or you can decide if your life will be directed in a negative direction. You are the creator and the controller, thus this process must be mindfully initiated by you; from within you; for you!

Do you have a high value of yourself?

If not, what is prohibiting you from having a higher value of yourself?

Notes:

Date:_____

AS LONG AS YOU CAN BREATHE YOU CAN BELIEVE AND YOU CAN ACHIEVE

This is an extremely powerful statement with major positive implications. However, many of us do not realize the power of our beliefs and how it affects every aspect of our lives. Whenever there is incongruency between our desires and the outcome of our lives, there is a fundamental misalignment of the inner working of our system of beliefs. Even if we decide within ourselves to continuously engage in disempowering, self-limiting and chaotic thoughts, there is still a strong belief present. This belief however, is not on positivity but is fixated on the belief in our disbelief. Our lives will continue to be filled with negativity, limitations and chaos because that is exactly what we believe is only possible in our lives.

"The manifestation of your life hinges upon a power within you that is impartial and unforgiving. There is only one prime directive; the execution of what you believe, regardless of whether this belief is constructive or destructive."

The true power of belief transcends the world as we know

it because it is one of the most powerful forces in the universe. It has the ability to create and also to destroy. Through the proper utilization of this power, we CAN create our lives according to what we are willing to believe. However, through the misuse of this power, we can also destroy our lives according to what we are willing to believe. The power of belief is equally implicit in the power of belief for good or bad. Our ability to make choices grants us the impartial ability to believe that our lives will be constantly filled with goodness or to believe that our lives will constantly be filled with pain and suffering. The impartiality of this ability to believe is encapsulated in the ability to believe itself. We must be extremely careful about what we believe or what we perceive is our only possible belief. For example, we may be under the impression that our beliefs are in harmony with our intentions, however, the true essence of our beliefs are filled with fear and frustration.

We are the authors of what we believe. Our beliefs will not automatically change in order to manifest our intentions. They will synchronize with whatever beliefs we continually foster in our minds. The resulting manifestation is only a mirror image of these beliefs. Belief itself is impartial; it does not account for our desires and intentions as a means of defining itself. In actuality, our beliefs are what define us; past, present and future. Our lives are typically a reflection of the various shades in between these beliefs. It is through our desire for fulfillment that we gravitate towards the beliefs that foster goodness in our lives. It is always our choice as it always is our choice...reword

All too often we fall victim to disbelief because we perceive that our lives are not moving in a desired direction or that it is not moving as quickly as we had intended. If we perceive that our lives are not progressing according to our desires, typically frustration will arise, indicating that the results of our actions are a direct violation of the required results of our intention. However, it is our chosen actions that are creating the actual results which are violating our desired results. Unfortunately, this frustration is typically not used for its intended purpose of providing constructive measurable feedback and thus creates additional frustration in our lives. Instead, we must use this frustration to affect a change in our beliefs so as to affect a change in our thoughts, which will affect a change in our actions.

Our physical capability must not be used as an undermining element of our belief. We can believe even though we may not be physically capable of performing certain activities, but the belief in ourselves will provide what is necessary for us to achieve our goal. As long as there is breath in our bodies, we possess the ability to believe. We may not be able to walk or speak, but we can still believe. For example, if you are not capable of physically accomplishing a task but you believe wholeheartedly that it will be accomplished; you will seek other alternatives such as locating others who accomplish these tasks for you so that you can still arrive at your goal. When we truly believe and are committed to this belief, we will continually seek ways to establish ourselves for success. Nothing will hinder us except the power of our disbelief.

Do you believe in the ultimate power of belief?

How can you foster belief in the receipts of your desires even if you are hindered physically?

Notes:

Date:_____

IT IS ONLY AS DIFFICULT AS YOU BELIEVE IT TO BE

Our beliefs and thoughts about every situation in our lives are what determine the *outcome* of every situation in our lives. These beliefs and thoughts influence how we perceive everything; from the bills in the mail to that new business being contemplated. Everything revolves around the type and magnitude of thoughts and the frequency of these thoughts. In fact, our entire "reality" is based on our beliefs and thoughts. The amazing part of this process is that we have the ability to change our reality simply by changing our beliefs and thoughts. Unfortunately, most of us do not realize the power that we have within us to affect a change in our lives. We are too busy focusing on life's perceived level of difficulty, while ignoring the small changes we can make to bring about a major reduction in this incorrect perception.

Every situation, every "dilemma" and every "problem" that we face can be classified and summarized by what our current beliefs and thoughts are at any particular moment in time. If our beliefs and thoughts are set in one particular direction, the situation, "dilemma" or "problem" will be perceived in a light that is relevant to our current beliefs and thoughts. Conversely, if our beliefs and thoughts are set in a different direction, the situation, "dilemma" or "problem" will be perceived in a totally different light or even may not be perceived as a dilemma or problem. In fact, based on our beliefs and thoughts, these so called dilemmas and problems may actually be perceived as opportunities depending on how they are viewed.

The more we believe that a situation is going to be difficult, the more difficulty will arise. The impetus for this outcome is that our focus is on the perceived level of difficulty, thus this is all we are able to see. All of the goodness and the opportunities that are right in front of us will go unnoticed because our focus is not on them. We always possess control over our perception of the level of difficulty. If we desire that our current situation becomes easier, then guess what; we must NOT only desire that it becomes easier but, _**we must intentionally believe it has already become easier because it is easily resolvable**_. Remember…there are always multiple alternatives to every situation. Unfortunately, most of us do not believe that we have other alternatives available and consequently make things more difficult through the introduction of self-created thoughts of limitation.

Any situation, no matter how severe it may seem, has a solution. When we absolutely believe that the situation is unsolvable, it becomes unsolvable because we are not searching for a solution. Thankfully, we can also choose to believe that the situation is solvable, since we always have options available. However, there must be a change in focus from the perceived difficulty of the "problem" to the enjoyment that a solution will bring. The answers will be revealed by focusing daily and methodically.

The world around us is perceived through our senses. Sensory information is subsequently transferred to our brain and is translated to create our perception of reality based on what we already believe. Our perceived reality causes us to produce subsequent "conclusive" thoughts based on this perception of reality. Each interaction that we have on a daily basis is acted out based on what we perceive, which is in turn based on what we believe. Everything is related to our perception of everything and also which perception we choose to place on it.

The senses used to perceive the external world are themselves jaded based on what we believe. Since our senses automatically filter out certain information based on our beliefs, our perception can become skewed because not only are we electing to process partial data from our senses, but our entire perception can be compromised based on the incomplete data it receives; the result of which produces an incomplete perception of reality. In principle, we must learn to move beyond our senses to create a new paradigm of possibilities.

The formulation and codification of our perception arises from the set of filters they pass through before becoming solidified. These filters are set in place by our beliefs and thus are not absolute. Yes…we do have a choice which filters we choose to select for our perception. Our beliefs actually define the filters through which the interaction with the outside world and the world inside of our minds are translated to form our reality. This is the reason our reality is based on our beliefs.

Every external or internal situation we encounter comes as a result of some previous belief, thought and action. The external "situations" that are experienced by us come in the form of information that we receive through our senses while the internal situations originate from a perception based on a dialogue between our conscious and subconscious minds. During an external situation, we are able to "see" how people respond to us; we "hear" negativity and we "feel" the pain of rejection in our lives which, in turn, further affects our beliefs, thoughts and actions. On the other hand, during an internal situation, the dialogue between the different types of thoughts that are allowed to foster in our minds produces the resulting actions that we take. Both scenarios come together to formulate the course of direction of our lives.

Whenever we choose to retain any negative conclusions based on the negativity of the past, we are constructing our beliefs based on these disempowering thoughts. Beliefs of nondeserving and not being good enough are but a few examples of the types of beliefs that generate the types of thoughts that impose a destructive dialogue with our constructive thoughts.

We have the power to decide how we interpret both our

external and internal situations. In fact, we have the power to decide what we believe and therefore shift the parameters by which our senses filter information to formulate our perception. Our beliefs create our internal and external situations and our perception of these situations is based on which set of filters we choose to define this perception.

When we are presented with any type of situation, we actually have "conclusive" interpretive thoughts that can render us powerful or powerless...all based on our current beliefs which are ultimately a derivative of our past experiences. Every situation, if viewed in a different light, will instantly morph into whatever light we decide to view it in. Therefore, if we choose to classify a situation as difficult, by definition it will become difficult. However, if we reclassify the same situation as simply constructive criticism or feedback to aid us in the adjustment of our current beliefs, we are opening our minds to the uncovering of opportunities in the current situation that was once perceived as difficult.

What situations in your life do you view as difficult?

How would your perception of the situation change by viewing it as an opportunity to improve some aspect of your life?

Notes:

Date:_____

YOUR LIFE IS BASED ON YOUR SPECIFICATIONS

Your life's specifications are a set of guiding beliefs you consciously or subconsciously set for yourself. These guiding beliefs influence your vision of success and ultimately create your life's experiences. Even if you desire a different outcome in your life, the specifics of your life will always be based on the specifics of the vision you adhere and continue to focus on in your mind. How do you see yourself? Do you love and respect yourself? Do you envision yourself living a life of abundance? If so, how often do you focus on this vision of success? The answers to these simple questions will mold who you are based on who or what you believe yourself to be. Amazingly, the answers to these questions are all defined by YOU. No matter what your past experiences were or what you believe others think of you, your life's specifications are set by what YOU believe and perceive. As a result, your actions will be directed by your thoughts and consequently your life will be directed by your beliefs.

All of your decisions are based on your beliefs and the perception driven by these beliefs. Since you are the author of your decisions, you must be willing to accept the consequences of selecting a limited specification for your life, if you choose anything but a life of success. Any time you feel as though it is impossible to achieve a life greater than your current specification, you must begin to evaluate what you currently believe. If you have core beliefs that denote an essence of non-deserving, doubt or fear, you will certainly believe that your current situation is the way that it should be. You will believe that you do not deserve a better life. You will doubt that you are able to achieve a better life and your fear based thoughts will cause you to create additional fear based thoughts in your mind, which will in turn affect your emotions and your actions. Thoughts of complacency, frustration and lack of motivation will run rampant in this type of environment. There is no wonder a vision of a life of success cannot survive; the conditions present are not conducive to its prosperity.

The reason for the initial discomfort has to do with the process of acclimating to this new way of thinking. Your fear based thoughts of change are part of a survival mechanism, but ironically you bring great harm to yourself through the elimination of a positive change in your life. Specify your life according to your own specification in order to specifically achieve true fulfillment in life!

In order for you to redefine your life's specifications, you must redefine your current beliefs. Even if a shift in your current belief system involves the exploration of uncharted waters, your focus must not be based on a fear of the unknown, but your focus must be fixated on the type of life you WILL enjoy as a result of the change. You are by no means the only person who has ever experienced what you are currently experiencing and you will not be the last. Others before you have been through far worse and have ascended to great heights. Remember, any change for the good is a good change, regardless of whether you are comfortable with it or not.

Do you believe that you have control over the results in your life?

Notes:

If so, why haven't you received your desires?

Date:_____

BELIEF IS THE PRESENCE OF FAITH IN THE ABSENCE OF PROOF

Our belief in our success is a chosen leap of faith. Faith denotes a belief in the presence of possibility in the absence of proof. It is perfectly normal to believe in something that we cannot physically see. This is quite evident in our daily experiences with usage of such things as electricity, gasoline, oxygen and so on. We cannot physically see their operation, but we believe in their performance. For example, we may not know how electricity works, but we are still willing to turn on the light switch because we believe that the light work. Likewise, we may not be able to physically see the element of belief, but we witness how it can improve our lives. This encompasses a leap of faith!

Our belief in our success may be intangible in the sense that we cannot physically touch and feel it, but it is mentally tangible in that we can "touch" and "feel" it in our minds. Once we construct a vision of success in our minds and have an "intimate relationship" with this vision, we are able to "touch" and "feel" it because it is real to us. The notion of using our imagination to create has long been dispelled and discouraged, in most cases, since childhood. In Principle, our ability to visualize and create our success in our minds is quelled through subsequent social and experiential conditioning. However, the resources available to regenerate our imagination still exist. It simply needs to be nurtured.

Since our success in the "real" world may seem intangible, what better place to formulate a tangible relationship with success than in our minds. However, most of us believe that if is far easier to believe in something that can be physically seen and touched than it is to believe in the untouchable. Ironically, we believe in the oxygen in the air around us and its ability to sustain us even though we cannot see or touch it. If we choose to refrain from breathing simply because we are not able to physically see or touch the oxygen in the air, we will surely die. Likewise, if we refrain from using our car or public transportation because we cannot see the gasoline exploding inside the engine, we will be relegated to walking or bicycling to work.

The reason we believe in the oxygen in the air and the safety of the gasoline exploding inside our engines is because there is a direct relationship that has been established. We believe in the ability of oxygen to keep us alive even though we have never seen it because we were able to witness to what it has done for us. We believe in our car's ability to transport us to and fro even though we have no idea of how the engine or transmission works. We do not ponder over the lack of proof, but we believe in the possibilities because the possibilities are evident to us on a daily basis. Likewise, the prior successes of others provide proof that other possibilities do exist and thus should strengthen our ability to succeed even though proof is not evident specifically in our lives.

All throughout history many have challenged the status quo to dispel their existing notions. The belief in the shape of the earth popularized by Columbus; the invention of the automobile and the first landing on the moon are but a few examples of how a belief in what appeared to be impossible and intangible proved to be a great success.

A vision of our success in our minds is just such a possibility in the absence of proof in the "real" world. If we can believe in the unknown intricacies of our automobile but still maintain confidence in its mobility, we should more so believe in the vision of our success. (Refer to Appendix IV). However, if we perceive that the effort required supersedes the applicable benefits, we will not engage in the process of creating and focusing on a vision of success. However, when we perceive that the benefits supersede the effort required, there will be a high level of commitment to our success.

Are you willing to believe in the possibility of your personal success?

How can you alter your current beliefs about your personal success in order to achieve this success?

Notes:

Date:_____

BELIEF MAKES ANYTHING POSSIBLE; BUT WITHOUT IT NOTHING IS POSSIBLE

Your life blossoms when you truly believe. It is exceptionally amazing how the mind unfolds and you begin to fully experience life when you begin to truly believe. Your mind and your entire life blossom only when you truly believe and this belief takes root in your very soul. Your ability to believe is governed by a choice to believe which unleashes an extremely powerful and creative force within you, through you and around you. Nothing can be accomplished without the presence of true belief, but with it anything can be accomplished.

Your level of believe is mainly based on your past experiences (experiential) and social domestication. When we were children, we believed very strongly in the "fantasy" world that we created in our minds through the use of our imagination. Unfortunately, prior to reaching adulthood, we were taught to limit the use of our imagination in this way. However, if we continued to create "fanciful" worlds in our minds, we probably would be committed to an insane asylum. But it is amazing to note that what is classified as "fanciful" is often what is disbelieved by the masses. Your vision of success may include a $10,000,000 contemporary home on 40 acres, but since the possibility of attainment is not shared by the masses, it is therefore deemed as "fanciful" and any further mention of it by you would be grounds for immediate extrication to a mental institution.

But is this the correct course of action for society? When we discontinue the use of our imagination and the creative abilities present and inherent in it, we lose a huge portion of our mental capacity and potential to create. Based on a "normal" and traditional interaction, the human mind reaches a perceived threshold of potential because there are certain elements we choose to accept as true and certain elements we choose not to accept as true. The elements that we accept as true are within themselves limiting because the elements we accept as true are limited. The elements we do not accept as true have limited our perception because we do not believe in them. If we intentionally released the chains of limitation and allowed our minds to expand beyond the current horizons, we would have to be willing to grant it the "extended" ability to believe once again in things beyond our "normal" mode of reality.

Every product that you see on a daily basis was once a belief and vision in the mind of its creator. This computer that I am currently using was once a belief and vision in someone's mind, as well as this chair that I am utilizing; this paper and pen that I am using; all were once beliefs and visions in someone's mind. If they chose not to believe in the vision that they created in their minds, than we probably would not have computers, chairs or paper to write on. We should be thankful that the individuals who possessed the vision of the things that we now enjoy in life actually believed in the realization of their vision.

When you believe in the vision of your success in your mind, it challenges the mind to seek ways and means to accomplish or bring into fruition what it believes is true and furthermore grants your mind the ability to fully blossom to its true potential. Without this belief, no effort would be expended and thus nothing will be realized and accomplished.

Can you imagine yourself as truly successful?

Do you wholeheartedly believe in this vision of success in your mind?

Notes:

Date:_____

THE SMALLEST IDEA CAN GROW INTO THE LARGEST IDEA

There are many examples in life that provide proof of this. For example, a small seed can germinate into a very large tree and small microscopic organisms can produce a human life. These are but a few of the examples of how something small can produce something big. There are thousands of other examples where something that appears to be small with a humble beginning can have a monumental affect. Initial size does not affect its ability to produce an end result that is many times the size of the original. The same principle applies to both negative and positive beliefs and thoughts. A small disempowering belief has the potential to mushroom into a cornucopia of disempowering thoughts based on fear and frustration. Likewise, a small empowering belief has the potential to completely change lives.

Each of us represents an idea of belief; an idea of what we deserve in life and an idea attached to the formulation of our self-worth. Since we are all ideas of what we were, are and will become, by the very changeable nature of an idea itself, we too can change. These ideas are constructed within our minds and therefore they can be destroyed within our minds. No idea of us is ever an immutable law. We have the ability to become as large as we can actually believe and perceive. There is no limit that can be set on our beliefs because they operate within the realm of our minds. No one has access to this information and no one can alter these beliefs unless we grant them access to our minds.

There is always room to build upon an existing idea or to completely destroy an old outdated idea and replace it with a brand new freshly remodeled idea. If we do not have belief and love for ourselves, we are classifying ourselves as the smallest idea based on a life of chosen limitation. On the other hand, when we choose to intentionally believe in greater possibilities for our lives and are mindful of our beliefs, thoughts and actions in relation to these beliefs, we are nurturing a seed that will eventually blossom into the largest idea of fulfillment, self-actualization and improvement for the greater good.

Even if we currently view ourselves as the smallest idea, we must realize that the smallest idea is not relegated to a life of remaining to be the smallest idea. It is what we do with this idea of ourselves that determines whether we will remain indefinitely as the smallest idea or mushroom exponentially into the largest possible idea. The path is open and available to us. We simply have to decide that we no longer desire to be the smallest idea based on a life of limiting beliefs; we desire to be the largest idea based on a life of possibilities! Our ability to achieve true fulfillment in life will depend heavily on our desire to transition from being the smallest idea to being the largest idea of possibilities. This smallest idea of ourselves based on what we have accepted as true does not have to determine the future outcome of our lives. However, what will determine the future outcome will be a decision to either remain as the smallest idea or to nurture this smallest idea until it blossoms into a massive idea that is bearing fruit for the benefit of ourselves and others.

With the correct nurturing and attention, we WILL blossom into the largest idea. This nurturing process involves first having love for ourselves. As we begin to love ourselves, we will also begin to believe in ourselves and truly value our life's desires. Actually, we may very well increase our level of desire beyond our wildest imagination. This increased belief and value will form the basis for the continued determination and commitment necessary to relentlessly find solutions that can transform our current "small idea" perception into "the largest idea" of possibilities.

Unfortunately, most are under the false assumption that what can be accomplished is dictated by others and your surroundings. This is so far from the truth. Your beliefs of what you can accomplish in your life are personally set by YOU and only YOU. Believe big and you will achieve great things!

Do you consider yourself to be a large or small idea?

How can you improve on the existing idea of yourself?

Notes:

Date:_____

BELIEVE FIRST... ASK QUESTIONS LATER

S hoot first and ask questions later brings back memories of the old western movies I watched as a child. Shooting first and asking questions later typically signifies a reversal of the "logical" progression of thought. You would think that in actuality one should ask questions first and then shoot later, if one decided to shoot at all. But there is an inherent belief that is buried deep within this sentiment. The person who shoots first proclaims dominance and control over the victim. The victim is not given a chance to engage the shooter and is subsequently at the mercy of the shooter.

Your willingness to believe takes on a similar definition. "Believe first and ask questions later" is a play on words but with a much more significant connotation. Every thought and every action carries with it the level of belief that was first used to construct it. The strength and the commitment of your belief are inherent on the strength and commitment of your thoughts and your actions. A strong belief that is accompanied by a strong commitment will produce strong thoughts and actions. There is no way to circumvent this truth.

How can you achieve anything if you do not first believe that you can achieve it? How can you think thoughts relative to your success if you first do not believe in your success? How can you receive if you do not first believe that you will receive? There are some instances where you may not initially believe wholeheartedly, but still actually achieve or receive your desires. In this case there is an element of subconscious belief that caused you to make the appropriate decisions that brought about your achievement or receipt of your desires. However, a life of continuous receipt will only come as a result of continuous belief and commitment to this belief. Belief is the primary element of every successful implementation of your goal. Therefore, to make your vision of success a reality, you must first not only believe that it is possible, but also believe that it is possible for you (Refer to Appendix IV).

Typically, the traditional course of action is to ask questions first in order to validate the possibility of believing. However, before you commit to believing in the receipt of your desires, the questions associated with the possibility of obtaining these desires must be answered initially within your mind. But this in itself is a method of casting doubt on the entire creative process. If you believe and know that anything you put your mind to can be accomplished by you and for you, you would automatically believe in your desires without casting a shadow of doubt by posing questions based on its possibility. Thus, the question of possibility is not necessarily a question of literal possibility, but is a question of personal possibility. Your desires are indeed possible because others have already received what you currently desire, however the question relates to whether your desires are literally possible for you.

Many people are too busy asking the questions what, when, where, why and how in order to produce that warm and fuzzy sensation that signifies an acceptance of surety of the possibility of their desires. "What steps am I going to take to get to my goal?", "When do I expect to get to my goal?", "Where are the things necessary to enable me to get to my goal?" are but a few of the questions that most may ask even prior to believing that their goal is actually possible. But what happens if you cannot immediately answer these what, when, where, why and how questions? This lack of knowing produces uncertainty in your mind, which in turn challenges your already fragile level of belief. When these types of questions are asked and the answers are not readily available, doubt in your ability to achieve your goal begins to enter your mind. This will begin to weaken an already fragile belief in your ability to achieve your goal.

Therefore, it is imperative that you first believe that you deserve your desires; you WILL receive your desires and you have the ability and the resources within and without to achieve your desires. When you truly believe in these elements and you focus intently on these elements, the what, when, where, why and how will begin to fall into place through your intense level of commitment and focus on your desires. If you focus intently on what you intentionally believe is possible, you will not only observe the answers that are already in front of you, but you will create the necessary solutions as well because your focus is on solution generation and not implicitly on the problem.

Do you typically believe first and ask questions later or do you ask questions first then decide on whether or not to believe based on your ability to answer all of your questions?

Why would you not decide to believe first in your desires?

Notes:

Date:_____

YOUR CURRENT PERCEPTION SIGNIFIES THE EXTENT OF YOUR BELIEF IN YOURSELF

Your current perception of yourself emanates from the level of belief in yourself. That being said, you can see how powerful and extremely important it is for you to ensure that you have the correct belief in yourself at all times. Your perception of yourself has been generated by the accepted beliefs from your past experiences. They have also been generated by what you have been taught and accepted to believe from others. Most, if not all of the scenarios where you were taught to believe and accept certain things as true most notably dates back to your childhood. For example, a parent may shout uncontrollably at a child when the child makes a "mistake" not realizing the detrimental effect that it will have on the child's life. This occurrence may form the basis for what the child subsequent believes and will continue to shape his or her reality.

The beliefs and thoughts that limit true potential in the present are beliefs and thoughts that have been formulated from the past. When you allow these limiting beliefs and thoughts of the past, coupled with your limiting thoughts in the present to create a vision of yourself in your mind, this vision will reflect the true extent of what you really believe about yourself; namely, a life filled with limitations. Limiting beliefs and thoughts that are retained eventually become the core focus and will eventually dictate what creates your reality, hence your experiences.

Since your actions are dictated by what you perceive as real, your limiting beliefs and thoughts will produce a limiting set of actions which will produce further limitations in your life. For example, if you perceive yourself as a failure, then it is because you believe that you are a failure. Likewise, if you perceive that you will be successful, it is because you believe that you will be successful. To counteract these limiting beliefs, you MUST intentionally believe in your success in order to perceive yourself as a success. Others will begin to treat you accordingly and increased opportunities will begin to flow your way as your focus changes from that of failure to the recognition and receipt of success. Likewise, others will only begin to treat you as though you are a failure when your actions are a direct replica of what you actually believe yourself to be.

It is important to note that positive belief without continuity and commitment will not produce the desired fruit. You must not only believe in yourself on a continuous basis, but you must also be committed to this belief and the attainment of your life of success. This commitment will provide you with the resources that will enable you to conquer the "obstacles" that are directly and indirectly created in your life.

All too often, we are out of touch with the vision of ourselves that we have created in our minds. Whether we want to admit it or not, each of us are a product of the types of beliefs and thoughts we had in the past and continue to have in the present. The main reason most of us do not believe in ourselves is because we spend most, if not all of our time focusing on the old limiting beliefs of ourselves. This negative perception is often so deeply rooted in the subconscious mind and continuously offers resistance to the production of a perception that is void of limiting beliefs. However, this negative perception can be replaced by intentionally transplanting a new positive perception in its place.

What is your current perception of yourself?

How can you change your perception of yourself in order to change your life?

Notes:

Date:_____

YOUR VISION OF YOURSELF IS CORRECT BECAUSE YOU SEE IN YOURSELF EXACTLY WHAT YOU BELIEVE YOURSELF TO BE

Each of us has a vision in our minds of what we believe ourselves to be. Our ultimate vision of ourselves, whether positive or negative, is typically based on a mechanistic view that is determined by the accepted beliefs we have amassed over a period of time. This vision is entirely correct because the way we "see" ourselves in our minds is exactly what we believe ourselves to be in the "real" world. This vision will affect every fiber of our lives! Who we are today is a byproduct of the cumulative effect of this vision over time. When we take a look at ourselves in our mind's eye, we are literally viewing a vision of ourselves in exactly the way we belief ourselves to be or should be.

Our system of beliefs is extremely powerful and defines exactly who we are and will become. If we were to change our current beliefs about ourselves by first identifying and altering our old antiquated beliefs, the vision of ourselves will also change. Thus, this new vision will be a new reflection of what we have chosen to believe ourselves to be. This new vision, whether positive or negative, becomes our new mental reference, but thankfully, we can change it at any time. Remember, whenever we alter our beliefs and perceptions of ourselves, the vision also changes to coincide and reflect the new belief.

The origin of our current beliefs has been constructed based on the accepted beliefs of the past. In order to redefine the vision of ourselves, we MUST:

— Fully define the core beliefs through the recapitulation process (Refer to Appendix III). Only then can we take steps to adjust these beliefs so that our thoughts, perception and actions will also change.

— Challenge and dispute these core beliefs for validity. Make the necessary adjustments to your core beliefs and define a new reference point for your life.

We are entirely at liberty to alter the direction of our lives by altering our beliefs and thus subsequently altering the vision of ourselves. After all, it is this vision that determines every aspect of our lives, including our thoughts, level of mindfulness or mindlessness, perception and our actions. Therefore, when we elect to change our old beliefs in order to produce a new and improved vision of ourselves, we automatically produce a new reference point of ourselves. All of our subsequent perceptions and thoughts will literally change because the reference point itself has changed. Now that you have a new reference point, your thoughts, perceptions and actions will change and therefore the outcome of your life will also change.

What current beliefs are interfering with your desired vision of success?

Through the process of recapitulation (Refer to Appendix III), how can you dispute these old beliefs?

Notes:

Date:_____

IF YOU DON'T BELIEVE THEN DON'T EVEN BOTHER

B elief is the key element for the achievement of anything that you desire. After all, if you do not believe then who will...right? If you do not believe in your life of abundance, then how can you possibly receive it? Your belief is the catalyst that provides the insight and the motivation that propels you towards completion. But beware! It is an intangible force that can either create or destroy. Even in the face of destruction, your belief is creating the destruction to which you are exposed.

Belief in what cannot be seen with the physical eyes is classified as faith. Belief in what can be seen with the "mind's eye" is classified as knowing. Undoubtedly, the use of your imagination is used to create a vision in your "mind's eye"; however, a true belief in this vision catapults it to the level of knowing. Without belief, your vision is simply a stagnant lifeless idea without momentum. However, belief used correctly is such a powerful ally and a great friend.

The things in your life that cannot be seen with the physical eyes are much more difficult to discern because you may have been conditioned to typically accept only what you can physically see, taste and touch. Anything beyond the boundaries of your five senses may be considered an anomaly and thus discarded. But your five senses only display a small part of the "realism" that surrounds you. You believe in electricity even though you cannot see it and likewise you believe in gasoline even though you cannot see it exploding inside your car's engine. Therefore, why do you doubt your ability to create and achieve success? The answer may reside in your lack of exposure to such success as a result of a disbelief in the possibility of this success.

You see, you have been exposed to electricity and the automobile since you were a child. Its presence is no great mystery to you even though its inner workings may still remain a mystery. You simply accepted that when you flicked the light switch you would receive light or when you turned the car key the car would automatically start as long as there was gas available in the tank. All of these exposures have solidified and made your belief in something that you cannot physically see more believable. If you did not believe that the light would come on or that the car would start, you probably would not even bother going through the motion. Likewise, the same principle applies in life.

Whatever your goals; whatever your desires; they will not have the full monumental effect of all of your energy resources than if you fully believed in yourself and your ability to achieve these desires. Even if you take the first initial steps without true belief, you will quickly become discouraged because you are missing the key element of true belief; that is a FOCUSED vision of your success in your mind. You will lose focus and will easily become dissuaded as soon as you hit a bump in the road. True belief automatically brings with it a high level of commitment and dedication to your success. Belief in the specific vision of success that you have created in your mind is the only way to give life to and bring this vision into reality. This is your vision so it is up to you to give it life though your belief and commitment in it! To do otherwise is simply an exercise in futility.

Do you fully believe in yourself and the merits of your current goal?

How will this belief aid in your success?

Notes:

Date:_____

TO TRULY KNOW IS TO TRULY BELIEVE; TO TRULY BELIEVE IS TO TRULY KNOW

In my life, I knew (or at least I thought I knew) that I was going to achieve my desires; however I neglected to truly believe in the receipt of these desires. I never executed the phrase "to TRULY know is to TRULY believe". I knew that I was going to be a success, however, I did not absolutely believe in the receipt of this success, therefore, I truly did not know. My absolute belief in the receipt of my success was marred by the limiting beliefs of non-deserving and not being good enough. Every time I began to build positive momentum, I would consciously and subconsciously sabotage my success by the actions that I selected based on my limiting core beliefs. At that point in my life, I never realized the true power of belief and how it created my world according to what I believed.

In order for you to truly know, i.e. possess an "intimate relationship" with the vision of success that is inclusive of your personal receipt of this success, you must absolutely believe in the possibility of this success and your personal receipt of this success (Refer to Appendix IV). The act of truly believing establishes the parameters by which the specifics of your vision of success are constructed. In other words, your level of belief determines the size and strength of the foundation upon which your vision of success is built. Therefore, when you truly believe in your success, your vision will be inclusive of this belief. In order to truly believe in the vision of success, you must take that necessary leap of faith and continue to intentionally interject beliefs and thoughts relative to the receipt of your success while intentionally eliminating thoughts of limitation and doubt. This process further solidifies the belief of success in your mind.

Believing and knowing have a symbiotic relationship in that they work with each other and for each other; they feed each other; they complement each other. If you are lacking in one area, it will adversely affect the other and vice versa. It does not matter where the deficiency resides; the overall result will be the same. If you believe but do not truly know within yourself that you will succeed, you do not truly believe and this will affect the outcome. Likewise, if you know, but do not truly believe in the vision of success, not only do you not truly know, but what you do "know" is not a complete reflection of the possibilities and this will also affect the outcome.

To truly know, you must rely on a vision of success that has been built on a foundation of true belief. A specific vision of success that is inclusive of true belief will not include the limitations and the limiting beliefs of the past, present or future. It will include anything and everything that you desire to receive in your life. Remember, this vision of success is created and designed by you and must not be based on the limiting beliefs and the social conditionings of others, but instead must be based on what you choose to perceive as possible through the use of your imagination. This vision must not rely on what you were conditioned to believe as humanly possible, but rather on what you choose to perceive as possible for YOU! Remember, many beneficial discoveries have been made throughout the centuries that have originally opposed the social norms only to disprove their validity; the shape of the earth and gravity are but a few examples. Whatever is possible will be set by the limits of your imagination.

When you truly believe, you will truly know that what

you believe will manifest itself into reality. Do not expect to accomplish your goal if you "know" that you will accomplish your goal but you do not absolutely believe. Do not expect to accomplish your goal if you "believe" that you will accomplish your goal but you do not truly know. If there is a lack in either one of the two, it will interject doubt and disbelief into your mind. This will affect your level of commitment causing you to quickly give up in the face of any adversity.

The manifestation process works, in part, by creating whatever you envision and focus on through solicited efforts to selectively choose actions that will bring about that which you maintain as your core focus. The belief that you have in the knowledge of your vision of success gives life to this vision. Otherwise, it is simply a vision that lacks the power of manifestation. Any vision possesses the ability to manifest itself based on the amount of belief and focus you give to this vision. If the vision you have of yourself is based on never being able to succeed and you continuously believe and focus on this vision, this is exactly what will be manifested in your life. A vision of continued poverty created by poverty conscious beliefs will create thoughts of continued poverty, resulting in a life filled with continued poverty. Just think, how can your actions promote wealth and success when your beliefs and thoughts are based on poverty and the creation of failure?

Do you truly know the specifics of your vision of success?

Was this vision of success built on a foundation of true belief?

Notes:

Date:_____

BY BELIEVING AND KNOWING AT ALL TIMES, YOU ARE AT ALL TIMES BELIEVING AND KNOWING

When you truly believe in the vision of your life as desired, you are actually giving life and vitality to your vision. You are taking every element of your being and committing it to what you believe. Your thoughts and your actions will substantiate and fulfill what you actually believe and perceive. This is the true power of manifesting your desires in your life. Knowing is actually a relationship you have with the vision of yourself and your success in your mind. When you create a vision of what you desire and actively interact with it, you KNOW that it exists because you KNOW that it exists in your mind. The knowledge and the ability of your desires to come to fruition MUST first arise from the knowledge you have of it in your mind and a strong belief in this knowledge. Ironically, all that you desire is already existing, however your lack of believe alters your perception to preclude only what you choose to perceive.

You will KNOW that your life will be fulfilling because you believe in your vision of success. In order for your vision of success to come into fruition, you must not only know that the vision exists but you must believe as though it has already materialized. Your vision of success cannot exist through a mixture of knowing and disbelief. Likewise, your vision of success cannot exist through the simultaneous existence of believing and not knowing. There must be a true belief and a true knowing at all times. Any deviation from this program, no matter how subtle it may seem, will begin to introduce resistance in your life and will alter your course of actions.

When you truly know and believe, the means to a positive resolution to your current situation will be revealed to you as a result of the creation in your mind and a change in your focus. The creation of your vision of success includes within it the specifics of your desired outcome. Now it is up to you to foster the correct amount of belief in this vision in order for you to make this vision a reality. When you know and believe that the outcome will be as created in your mind, you will not be frustrated with the little hiccups along the way. You will begin to view the hiccups as feedback which will aid you in redefining your overall process, knowing and believing that the final outcome will be attained according to your desires. The hiccups may be a manifestation of submerged thoughts of disbelief that are offering resistance in your life. When there are no hiccups along the way, this may be an indication that things are going according to plan. However, do not neglect to continuously analyze your beliefs, thoughts and actions to ensure that they are still in harmony with your objectives.

The major reason the outcome of our lives is not in accordance with our vision of success can be directly traced to the presence of disbelief. Another impetus for the inconsistency resides in our use of frustration and the fearful thoughts we allow to permeate our minds. Your vision of success requires a specific course of action in order to attain this vision of success. When you allow the frustrations, fears and false perceptions to alter your beliefs, thoughts and actions, further fear and frustration are automatically produced and the outcome will be different from your desired vision of success. In Principle, mindfulness is not just an exercise; it is a lifestyle of continuous application. You must be mindful when you eat, shower, work, play and sleep. Mindfulness must encompass every aspect of your life. Even a slight deviation from your specified plans such as a subtle decision to err on the side of instant gratification, will produce experiences that will affect your life.

Do you believe and KNOW your vision of success?

Are you mindfully monitoring your beliefs, thoughts and actions to ensure they are meeting the requirements for your success?

Notes:

Date:_____

WHEN YOU SETTLE IN LIFE, LIFE GIVES YOU EXACTLY WHAT YOU SETTLED FOR

You receive out of life exactly what you accept and settle for in life. When you believe in the self-created and accepted limitations in our lives, you are literally performing a disservice to yourself and others. You will not be able to see beyond the limitations that you have set for ourselves or have allowed others to set for us. These limitations that you set in place or allow will produce the maximum threshold for all of the possibilities that you experience in our lives. Settling in life can be accomplished with the greatest of ease, especially when our focus is on the "problem" and not on the solution to the "problem". If you continue to focus exclusively on the "problem", naturally you will never find a solution because it is not part of your focus.

A "problem" that is continuously a "problem" will eventually be perceived as a "normal" and acceptable function of your everyday life as you begin to believe that your alternatives are extremely limited. You then begin to settle, whether consciously or subconsciously, for the occurrences in life that you perceive are at the maximum threshold of our capabilities. Since you perceive that there are no other alternatives available, the only logical course of action in your mind is to settle.

However, when you settle in life, what you settle on is exactly what you will receive and continue to receive! The bar of possibilities has been lowered thus disallowing the recognition of opportunities that will propel you beyond your current threshold limits. The alternatives and opportunities are right in front of you; but your limitations have blinded you from its revelation.

Even though there are solutions, alternatives and opportunities right before you, you will not recognize them as such because your perception has been skewed towards a mechanistic belief that inherently includes massive traces of limitations. The limitations that you have established for yourself will become the basis for your perception and thus your reality. When you perceive of anything as impossible to achieve based on a predetermined limited view, you will automatically disavow the existence of anything greater. Thus, the existence of anything greater than your perceived limitations will not occupy your life.

Inherent in all humanity is the desire to achieve that which only can be believed and perceived by the human mind. To attempt to achieve that which is deemed impossible is simply a violation of this premise. Many times, others may view your desires as impossible. However, as long as your view is fixated on the possibility of your desires, there will be a yearning to receive your desires, because they are "real" to you. In Principle, it is imperative that you are not seduced into the temptation of settling in life.

When you are tempted to settle in life, you must refute this temptation at all cost. Settling in life only motivates you to further accept the limiting beliefs of the past as perpetually "real" and "true". You have the power to choose to settle and therefore you have the power to choose not to settle! Even though a situation may seem difficult, if you remain mindful and continue to focus on solutions and alternatives, you will quickly realize that you are not relegated to settling in life.

The ability to receive your desires is disabled by the massive collection of limiting beliefs that you harbor in your mind! However, you will achieve and receive your intended desires if you focus intently with determination and commitment. Limiting beliefs, which automatically breed fear and frustration, must never be introduced into your mind.

Have you currently settled in life?

How can you change your beliefs to remove your limiting threshold?

Notes:

Date:_____

TO NEED AND TO WANT IS TO CONTINUE TO NEED AND TO WANT

Our perception of what we either need, want or desire is based on our belief in our ability to achieve and receive what we need, want or desire. A perception based on a need, want or desire also relates to the direction of our focus in relationship to our needs, wants or desires. However, the caveat here resides in the subtle differences between the philosophy of needing and wanting versus desiring. There are major subtleties inherent in both philosophies, but the implications are astounding. A need refers to a lack of something and similarly a want refers to a suffering from the lack of something. Clearly both definitions depict a focus on lack as opposed to focusing on abundance. However, a desire refers to an expression of a wish or request. The focus on lack is not the prime directive but a wish or request for the item desired.

Any time we express a need or want, we are admitting to ourselves and our creative abilities that our focus is on the lack of what we perceive we need or want. The inherent tenet here is actually a disbelief in our ability to create what we desire. The impetus for not affirmatively stating that we are going to receive X for example, is because we do not truly believe that we will receive X. However, if we alternatively state affirmatively that we are going to receive or we have already received, we are stating our affirmation with absolute confidence and belief in the receipt of our desires. How else can we receive our desires if we do not truly believe that we will receive them? Focusing consciously or subconsciously on lack will inherently make lack the core focus. This lack subsequently becomes a fundamental part or bases for our reality.

We may also conclude that since our lives exhibited traits of lack in the past, it will continue to exhibit traits of lack in the present and the future. The common consensus now becomes the common question, "Why struggle to achieve when I probably will not receive it?" The reason for this question stems from a belief that our lives will continue to have the same amount of lack as it did in the past.

Frustration and fear are always a byproduct of focusing on lack whereas exultation and enthusiasm are always a byproduct of focusing on abundance. Unfortunately, the terms wanting and needing have become so intertwined within our vernacular that they require a specific mindset to consistently become aware of their usage. The subtle destruction that they impose is rarely conceptualized and thus continues to run rampant.

The frustration and fear associated with needing and wanting prohibits a life filled with recognizable alternatives and solutions. The fact that we may view something as impossible to attain is merely a perception on our part. There is never only one available alternative. There is an abundant supply of available options. It is merely our belief and our focus that distorts our view. It causes us to believe that what we actually desire is not possible and attainable and therefore must be reclassified as a need or want. Furthermore, the use of such phrases as "I need to have this" instead of "I am going to have this" or "I want this" instead of "I am going to receive this" all depict our level of disbelief. If we believe that our current life is a mirror image of the past, filled with needs and wants, this is the reality that we are creating and our thoughts and actions will make it so because this is our belief and this is our focus.

Is your focus fixated on a need, want or desire?

Do you view the importance of having a desire versus needs and wants?

Notes:

Date:_____

DO NOT ASK FOR WHAT YOU DO NOT DESIRE TO RECEIVE

In the "real" world, no one makes a request for something they do not desire or do they? Most of us do not desire to intentionally bring negative circumstances into our lives nor do we relish the thought of such experiences. But, what actually occurs when we have a desire for a life of abundance and fulfillment but receive otherwise? What happens when we desire a life of joy and happiness but we continually receive a life of pain and misery? Is it that we are innately predestined with "bad luck" or is it that the "world is against us"?

The experiences in your life come as a direct or indirect result of the mental vision of yourself that was created by your past and present beliefs of and in yourself. In other words, the experiences in your life are a direct and indirect reflection of the image you create consciously and subconsciously in your mind! Please note that the vision of you is built upon your acceptance or rejection of certain belief principles. For example, a desire for a life of success does not automatically produce this success unless there is a clear vision of success built on a foundation of strong belief and an acceptance of the receipt of nothing less. Take the time to "review" the vision of yourself in your mind. What do you see? Where do you see yourself in the next few days, months or even years? What do you envision as possible or impossible? What past negative experiences are intricately intertwined within this vision? What "little voices" do you have in your mind that affects this vision? These are some of the questions to ponder as you take a glimpse at the person you have chosen to create in your mind.

The underlying impetus for everything that you say and do rests on this vision. This vision directly and indirectly affects your thoughts and actions by influencing and controlling them with the ultimate purpose of actualizing this vision. For example, if you view yourself as "unlucky" and focus continually on this vision, your thoughts and actions will be based on fear. Your desire may be to have a life filled with good fortune, but your vision exemplifies a life filled with "bad luck" and continued misfortune.

Consequently, your subsequent actions are based on your fearful thoughts, which ironically possess no true intent or purpose towards the specific goal of good fortune. "Why even try to bring good fortune into my life when I know that I will always have bad luck?" you surmise. Therefore, you neglect to focus on the specific intentions that are related to the receipt of good fortune. Your decisions are not based on the attainment of good fortune, but are based on a fear of bad fortune. Since fear is blinding, you will not "see" the opportunities for good fortune in your life because your focus is entirely on the perceived bad fortune. In Principle, your thoughts and actions will only be based around the limitations of what you can "see"; bad fortune.

You are literally requesting and creating that which you do not desire. The vision of yourself that is created in your mind will be executed whether you desire it or not. This vision is literally your mental program that defines how you process your life. Even when you have a vision of your life as being filled with "bad luck", but possess a conscious desire for "good luck", the elements of manifestation are present. You believe in this vision of "bad luck" because it is perceived that your life has always been filled with "bad luck". You are focused intently on this vision of "bad luck" because it dominates your thoughts and emotions. Therefore, your life will manifest that which you believe and bestow your attention, even if you desire otherwise.

Unfortunately, the vision of ourselves is generally not reviewed for errors and typically exists in a form that is not "readily" discernible until we choose to live our lives based on mindfulness. We have not been trained to purposely create a vision of our actual desires based on a high level of belief; therefore, we live at the mercy of whatever vision that has been surreptitiously created within our minds. A vision that is not specifically created based on a belief and desire for fulfillment is a vision that has been automatically generated based on the belief and acceptance of the negativity of the past.

Each day that we retain a vision of success based on absolute belief and focus on it daily, we are daily inviting that which we believe and desire to enter our lives. Conversely, each day that we retain a vision of "bad luck" or any other type of negative vision about ourselves, our daily focus is on the perceived negativity, fear and lack and as such we are daily inviting that which we believe but do not desire to enter our lives.

Now that you have read this chapter, have you discovered that you have asked for what you do not desire to receive? If this is the case, I encourage you to refer to the opening remarks of this chapter and ponder its meaning. May the end results of your search be that when you ask for your desires and truly believe in the success of receiving them, your life becomes abundant.

What is your current vision of success?

Is this vision inclusive or exclusive of your actual desires?

Notes:

Date:_____

YOU WILL RECEIVE ONLY WHAT YOU BELIEVE YOU DESERVE

You will receive ONLY what you believe you deserve! This is a fundamental principle of life and is deeply rooted in the level of belief in your ability to create your life the way you desire. The ability to create a life of either positivity or negativity stems from the use of creative visualization (the process of creating a vision of this positivity or negativity as it relates to you) and is directly affected by your belief in what you deserve. If you believe that you do not deserve to drive a luxury car or live in a fancy home, you will not be able to create a truly believable vision of that in your mind. If you cannot create a truly believable vision of your success in your mind, then how can you achieve it?

There is a huge difference between living a life based on a desire and living a life based on a choice. Desires are what you hope to achieve and receive, but it is ultimately the choices that you make that determine whether or not your desires will come to fruition. You may have a desire of living a life of great wealth and happiness however your limiting beliefs will interfere with your choices which will inevitably sabotage your life.

The reason a life of lack is so much easier to create than a life of abundance is because the core belief and focus is on a life of lack instead of a life of abundance. This life of lack is all that is habitually known and accepted as "normal". The predetermined limitations have created more thoughts of lack than thoughts of abundance. This creates a volume of negative thoughts which outweigh the volume of positive thoughts and eventually forms a reality of perceived possibilities. Thus, the vision that is created is based on this falsely perceived negativity. You can always determine the direction of your life by comparing the amount of negative beliefs and thoughts to the amount of positive beliefs and thoughts that are flowing through your mind.

Your beliefs and thoughts about what you deserve typically stem back from your childhood experiences. Ultimately, your belief in what you think you deserve stems from your acceptance of certain principles based on your past experiences. If you accept the limitations set forth by others, what you believe you deserve will also be limited. Typically the common dogma is to shun the notion of deserving because it is often miscategorized as immoral. But since the luxury cars were designed to be purchased and you have the legal means of purchasing such a car without disrupting your life or the life of others, then by all means you deserve that fancy car. What you believe you deserve should not have any artificial limits imposed upon it as long as it does not negatively affect your life or the lives of others.

Deserving not only includes finances but it includes all aspects of our lives. It encompasses relationships, health, happiness and so on. Whatever you believe you deserve will set a threshold on the upper limit of what you will receive in all of these areas. How can you truly obtain a life of financial freedom, healthy relationships and good health when you do not believe that you actually deserve to have these things in your life? It is certainly a contradiction to desire certain things in your life while simultaneously believing and thinking that you do not deserve the very things that you desire in life.

Your beliefs and thoughts are specifically a combination of (a) your own beliefs and thoughts and (b) the accepted beliefs and thoughts imposed by others. Therefore, if you have a vision of what you desire in your mind while simultaneously believing that you deserve to reap the benefits of this vision, you will create ways to make this vision a reality. This process is at the very core of the creative processes in your mind. You must not only create, but you must also believe that you will enjoy what you have created in your mind. Ironically, many people believe that they deserve everything that life has to offer, but they cannot envision their desires nor interact with them in their minds. The result of this is an attitude of deserving but a lack of motion towards what they believe they deserve due to the presence of disbelief. All things are possible if you believe; believe and all things will be possible.

Do you believe that you deserve to attain all of your desires?

If not, how do your past experiences promote feelings of non-deserving?

Notes:

Date:_____

WHAT YOU BELIEVE SOLIDIFIES THE "TRUTH" THAT YOU EXPERIENCE

W hy is it that we become frustrated when faced with an undesired situation? Ironically, many of us do not even realize that we are frustrated until it is no longer possible to deny this fact. This frustration is typically created when the outcome of our lives is different from what we desire. However, the reason for this difference stems from a lack of belief that the outcome WILL be in harmony with what we desire. This is further compounded by a belief in our lack of control and the unavailability of other alternative options. These types of beliefs are limited and inherently limiting. They automatically set the tone for a life filled with limitations. Unfortunately, when we deliberately limit ourselves and our abilities by choosing to believe in limitations, we are performing a grave disservice through the creation of a limited life filled with limited experiences.

The major portion of our frustration is created as a result of continuously focusing on the "problem" at hand and how it affects us emotionally instead of focusing intently and continuously on a solution to the "problem". Focusing on the "problem" is tantamount to focusing on the lack thereof; therefore, when we spend our precious time focusing on the "problem", our minds are fixated on the perceived lack thereof. Eventually this pattern of behavior begins to constitute the formation of our "reality". For example, when the bills arrive in the mail, we typically begin to focus on the perceived lack of money available for us to satisfy these bills. Notice that I said perceived lack of money available. Available money does not necessarily represent money that is in a bank account. It can represent money that is available through other means such as overtime or tag sales. The perceived lack thereof is conceptual because the focus is based intently on a limited point of view. This limited point of view is fixated on only one conclusion; there are insufficient funds in the bank account to satisfy the bills. This perception does not take into account other alternatives that are readily available. Therefore, this perceived lack is based on a limited perception and WILL create the limiting experiences in our lives.

The perceived lack of financial control only serves to generate fear and frustration which further generates more fear and frustration. As long as we live in a society that prides itself on convenience, there will be bills in the mail. We need such things as electricity, insurance and telephone, thus we will always have bills in our mailbox. However, it is our perception of these bills compared to our perceived lack that renders us seemingly powerless. When we perceive that we are in control and have other alternatives available to us, we will not focus on the bills themselves but we will turn our attention to the creation of additional sources of income that will enable us to more than satisfy these bills.

This example defines a huge part of a lack of mindfulness. The "lack" in our lives is always a perceived lack because we define whether or not "lack" exists in our lives. Since everything in our lives is based on our perception, the perceived "lack" that we are experiencing may not even exist. But it is what we believe that solidifies the "truth" that we experience. If we were to alter our beliefs and thoughts, our perception too will change and the perceived lack will disappear. This comes as a result of being ever so mindful of our frustrations, while continuously and preemptively focusing on the solutions exclusively.

When we dedicate our time to focus continuously on

absolutely believing in our success, our subsequent decisions and actions will change to reflect and justify these beliefs that we hold as true. Our lives will then begin to move in accordance with those beliefs that we hold intently and continuously in our minds. **Truly believe in the <u>inability</u> to achieve success and that will be the "truth" we will experience. Conversely, if we truly believe in our <u>ability</u> to achieve success and fulfillment, we will create a different "truth" that will lead to a successful experience.**

Can you identify the direct correlation between your be-liefs and your experiences?

What changes can you make to your beliefs in order to change your experiences?

Notes:

Date:_____

ALL THINGS ARE POSSIBLE IF YOU BELIEVE; BELIEVE AND ALL THINGS ARE POSSIBLE

E verything in your life is only limited by the limitations YOU place on it in your mind. Thus, the limitations set forth affect your ability to perceive of anything beyond the scope of these limitations. Therefore, when you perceive that something is improbable or impossible, you will not make every effort to achieve it. Everything is based on your power of belief because it is your belief that either creates the possibilities or the impossibilities in your life.

I recall a conversation with a young lady who told me that she could not see herself as being wealthy because she never believed that it was possible. Her belief was based on the observation of the lifestyle of her parents, family, friends and her environment. Her parents, friends and family were not wealthy nor were they ever exposed to others with wealth. In fact, she stated that her parents, family and friends were all struggling just to "make ends meet" and have been doing so as long as she could remember. Thus, she believed that her chances of becoming wealthy were relatively slim if not impossible because the attainment of wealth had been eliminated from her possibility matrix (Refer to Appendix IV). Therefore, the outcome of her life will be dependent on the belief that she has in the possibility and her ability to attain wealth. Since she did not believe in her eventual attainment of wealth, she will not produce thoughts related to her success and therefore her actions will not promote her success. She will not seek to create opportunities for success nor will she be able to identify opportunities that are already available to her, because her focus is not on her success; rather it is on her perpetual lack. Since all things are possible, a change in her focus as a result of a change in her beliefs will produce a change in her thoughts and actions, thus making it possible for her to receive.

This example is a classic view of how many of us conduct our everyday lives. When we have consistent thoughts of "making ends meet", we naturally believe that a life of success in the future is beyond our reach. The limitations that we possess in our lives are as a result of the limiting beliefs that we have chosen to accept and continue to foster in our mind. This is why they are called limiting beliefs. These limiting beliefs WILL limit every possible aspect of our lives. Amazingly, the limiting beliefs that we had in the past and currently have in the present are simply perceptual ideas. They are not immutable and thus can be changed. However, when we value the fact that our lives are based solely on the possibilities that we create within our minds, we will constantly seek to remove the limitations from our beliefs and as such the limitations will be removed from our lives. There is nothing to lose by believing in ourselves but we stand the risk of losing everything if we continue to disbelieve.

What are your current limiting beliefs?

How can you change these beliefs to remove the limitations from your life?

Notes:

Date:_____

BELIEF AND SYSTEMATIC THOUGHT PATTERNS ARE WHAT MAKES ONE TRULY SUCCESSFUL

You cannot have ultimate success in your life if you do not truly believe in yourself and your ability to attain this success nor can you have ultimate success in your life if you do not have a systematic thought process that fosters thoughts of success and only success. The beliefs and thoughts generated from these beliefs will determine your actions on a daily basis. Consequently, your actions will determine the direction of your life. Understand the extreme importance of these statements and you will be well on your way to attaining what you desire in life.

Success is entirely subjective and can come in many forms. Success for one individual may not be success for another. However, regardless of what constitutes success in your life, the common denominator for each and every form of success is belief in the attainment of this success. The difference between you and others who have the type of success that you desire is that their level of belief in the possibility of success, their belief in their ability to ultimately succeed and their systematic thought patterns are either markedly or subtly different from yours. It does not matter what you choose to accomplish in your life; all that matters is that you truly believe that it is possible to attain and you truly believe in yourself and your abilities to attain and receive what you desire.

True belief automatically initiates a systematic thinking process. When you believe, your thoughts and actions are linked to these beliefs and the outcome will ultimately be based on these beliefs. When you believe that there are always alternatives available to you, this belief will keep you fueled even when you are faced with unexpected obstacles. Your belief and your commitment will create the determination that will help you to locate or create other alternatives to get you to your goal, regardless of the circumstances.

Your systematic thought process is an active plan that encompasses the plan of action for your life. Nothing worthwhile can be accomplished without a plan of action. It is extremely important to note however, that belief is always a prelude to a plan of action. You would not produce a set of plans unless the objective of the plan was deemed possible. For example, before you take a vacation, you engage in the planning process; before you purchase a home you engage in the planning process and before you send your kids off to college or plan for retirement, you engage in a planning process. If there was disbelief in the possibility of taking a vacation, buying a home or retirement, you would probably not plan for these events because they would be deemed as impossibilities.

Your systematic plan of action must include the types of beliefs, thoughts and actions that are required to attain what you desire. The elements of your plan must be held constantly in the forefront of your mind and must be the highlight of your focus. Through the use of mindfulness, you must use the requirements of this systematic plan of action to constantly compare the required beliefs, thoughts and actions with your current beliefs, thoughts and actions. When you are mindful, you will immediately notice any deviation in your beliefs, thoughts and actions from the requirements of your plan. This is your opportunity to fine-tune your current beliefs, thoughts and action to bring them back in line with the requirements of your plan.

Why do we risk un-fulfillment in our lives by neglecting

to construct a plan of action that is free of limitations? Here again, it relates to what we believe is possible for our lives. Ironically, we choose to believe that we will be able to take a vacation; send the kids to college or plan for retirement, but we choose not believe that we will be able to attain all that we desire in life. Our minds are filled to the brim with limitations in all shapes and sizes and thus we are never able to actualize our vision of success because of a lack of belief.

What is your systematic plan of action?

Is this plan of action based on what is required to achieve your desires or is it riddled with fear and disbelief?

Notes:

Date:_____

BELIEVE YOU ARE SUCCESSFUL AND YOU WILL BE SUCCESSFUL AT ATTRACTING SUCCESS

S uccess in your life comes as a result of successfully thinking thoughts of success. By thinking thoughts based on fear, frustration and doubt, you are thinking thoughts based on the opposite of success. When you think thoughts based on the opposite of success, this is exactly what you will receive; the opposite of success. Since your thoughts are what dictate your actions in life, it only stands true that to have the desired success in your life you must be successful at maintaining thoughts of success in your mind.

The process of thinking successfully embodies a lifestyle of believing and focusing on specific thoughts that are intentionally geared towards your goal. The way that you can ensure that you are constantly thinking successfully is to constantly focus on the vision of your success that you have created in your mind through the use of your belief in this success. The way that you ensure that you are continually focusing on this vision of success is through the use of mindfulness to monitor your thoughts, emotions and action on a daily basis to ensure that they relate to the attainment of your vision of success. Both mindfulness and your vision of success are directly related to each other and their peaceful coexistence serves to produce and promote balance and harmony in your life.

The way to be ever so mindful of your thoughts is to initially embrace the awareness that negative beliefs and thoughts WILL have a negative impact on your life. Anytime you have a negative thought, there is a negative emotion associated with this thought. However, through the use of mindfulness, you can readily detect the presence of these negative thoughts simply by remaining in touch and in control of your emotions. Our emotions are a great indicator of whether we are happy, sad or indifferent. When we are happy, we are predominantly thinking positive thoughts, however, when we are sad, we are predominantly thinking negative thoughts. Thus, our emotional state acts as a barometer for both our conscious and subconscious beliefs and thoughts.

To rectify the negativity associated with negative thinking, we must first calm our minds and subsequently analyze our current thoughts, identify the originating beliefs of these thoughts and question its validity. When we identify the beliefs that are creating these disempowering thoughts, we must focus on refuting and eliminating these invalid beliefs. By deliberately introducing empowering beliefs into your mind, you are increasing your current level of belief and thus increasing your level of empowering thought, which in turn solidifies your belief (Refer to Appendix IV). When your level of belief begins to increase, everything related to your belief will also increase. Your positivity, commitment, focus etc. will all increase in correlation to the increase in your belief. Thus, by participating in intentionally believing on a daily basis, your intentional thoughts will eventually become habitual and you will find yourself believing and thinking thoughts of success. You will immediately notice a change in your emotions and your actions. The level of success received will be commensurate to this increase in your level of belief.

Is believing and thinking thoughts of success a part of your daily diet?

How can you decrease your negative thoughts and increase your positive thoughts so that you can attract success in your life?

Notes:

Date:_____

KNOW THAT YOU ARE AND WILL BE EVERYTHING THAT YOU TRULY DESIRE

B eing everything you truly desire to be goes beyond just having a basic desire. The complete process encapsulates not only "knowing" that your desires will come to fruition, but also encompasses a committed belief in the "intimate relationship" you have established with the vision of success in your mind. It is simply not enough to embrace a basic version of "knowing" with the expectation of receiving your desires. There must be a complete "knowing" that is based on your absolute belief in yourself and your ability to accomplish your goals.

When you unequivocally know that you are or will be everything that you desire, you will have unshakeable belief and commitment in the vision of your ultimate success. Know then, that the extent of your beliefs and thoughts and the extent of the vision that you have of yourself, will dictate the extent of what you will become. The power to create your life is working in full force regardless of whether your beliefs, thoughts and vision are constructive or destructive. Thus, even if your desires are contrary to your beliefs, thoughts and vision, the creation of your life ultimately hinges on the belief contained in the vision you retain and focus on in your mind. However, many of us do not realize that every day; what we believe, what we think and what we "see" of ourselves in our mind are actually creating our current experiences, thus creating what we will eventually become! This is the power that we all possess.

It does not matter if you desire to live a life of abundance; if this life of abundance is not created and retained within your mind as a vision of your success and you are not focused intently and continuously on this vision, you will NOT receive your life of abundance. The actual outcome will coincide with whatever vision you hold, regardless of your desires. Thus, your desires will be ineffective and futile unless you create and maintain an undiluted and exact vision of what you desire and mix this recipe with heaping amounts of belief and commitment to this belief. For example, a villain can be successful in his villainy because even though his goals are negative, he possesses strong beliefs of possibility and commitment to his negative goals.

You must first believe in the positive vision that you have created and hold it clearly and consistently in your mind in order to materialize your desires. You must subsequently think thoughts that are conducive to the accomplishment and attainment of these desires. Once you begin to think thoughts related to the attainment of your desires and you consistently retain the vision of your success in your mind, the initial belief that you have in your ability to accomplish these desires will dramatically increase. Your "knowing" and your belief in this "knowing" are constantly working in concert to direct your thoughts, emotions and actions to do everything that is necessary to receive what you envision. At this point, you will know and believe that you are or will be everything that you desire because everything that you desire is inclusive in your vision of success.

There is a universal continuous search for wholeness and completion. Some of us are searching for love and affection, while others may be searching for appreciation and respect. This perceived "missing" piece of the puzzle dominates our every thought and action which creates the environment of perceptions in which we interact. However, if we mindfully recognized the benefits and embraced the importance of the

creative process in our minds, we would quickly seek to eliminate the disempowering thoughts that are creating the void
in our lives and immediately take steps to revamp the vision
of ourselves that we "see" in our minds. The void associated
with love, affection, appreciation and so on, is directly associated with the void that we create in our minds. For example,
a belief based on the impossibility of ever receiving true love
and affection will produce the harsh reality of never receiving
true love and affection. Remember, we will bring into reality
that which we know and believe to be true.

What do you desire to accomplish in your life?

_____

_____

Do you have a vision of this desire in your mind?

_____

_____

Notes:

_____

_____

_____

_____

_____

_____

Date:_____

THOUGHTS

I BELIEVE IN THE POWER OF THOUGHT BECAUSE IT IS MY THOUGHTS THAT DEFINE WHO I AM AND WILL BECOME

Our thoughts defined who we were in the past, who we are in the present and who we will become. They define who we currently are because they are directly affected by our perception of everything. Our perception based on our beliefs is what causes us to think and act in a certain way. Our thoughts define and affect who we will become because one thought leads to the creation of another similar thought.

Just imagine, you can completely redefine who you are by changing the thoughts that define you. Specific thoughts will bring about specific results and through the process of association will solidify your current beliefs and perceptions, which will produce more thoughts of the same. If you define the type of person you desire to become and begin to focus on believing and thinking the thoughts that are specific to that type of person, you will become that person.

This is the ultimate power of our thoughts. Whether we are aware of it or not, we are defining and redefining our lives with each and every thought. In most cases we lament on our current circumstances without realizing that it is our thoughts that have brought us to this point in the first place. Unfortunately, when this occurs, we believe that our options are too limited for us to think otherwise because we are literally blinded by the limitations set forth in our mode of believing and thinking.

So, how do we change the thoughts that define who we are? The answer relates to a desire to transform ourselves into what we truly desire. Once an absolute decision is made to bring about a change, we must constantly monitor our beliefs, thoughts and emotions to ensure that they do not reinvigorate our residual antiquated beliefs. This is the premise of mindfulness; monitoring our thoughts and emotions constantly and subsequently making a decision to immediately replace the negative thoughts with positive thoughts through a change in our core beliefs. The process will become habitual as we continue to focus on mindfulness, submerging ourselves in the process of eliminating our negative and limiting beliefs while fostering the creation of positively empowering beliefs.

We will become who and what we desire because we will be completely redefined through our continued focus on the correct beliefs, thoughts and actions.

Do you believe in the power potential of thought?

Do you believe in this power potential of your thoughts to change your life?

Notes:

Date:_____

I AM WHATEVER I THINK I AM

An immense amount of power is embedded in this statement. At your very core are beliefs and thoughts that not only color your life, but also directly dictate it. Every thought, every emotion and every action in the past, present and future is solely based on how you perceive yourself and your surroundings. This personal perception is based on the image of yourself that you hold in your mind. This mental image itself is based on the beliefs that you accept as true from your past experiences and the beliefs that you accept as true based on the interactions with your surroundings.

Your thoughts and actions are controllable because they are derived in some way, shape or form from your beliefs, which too is controllable. Some of these thoughts and actions may occur as a result of a conscious effort while others may occur as a result of a subconscious effort. Even though they may occur as a result of subconscious efforts, they are still being generated by your mind and as such belong to you. Even when your thoughts are not known to you on a conscious level, they are known to you on a subconscious level. Simply because you may not be able to presently tap into the true essence of your subconscious does not preclude the fact that these thoughts are being produced by YOUR subconscious mind.

Through practice you can effect a change in your current beliefs and thoughts to create a new you. You can change the current image of yourself to create the new you that you have always desired. The current image of yourself has been developed over the years as a result of the assimilation of past experiences. Your core beliefs have defined what you are willing to accept as true and what you are willing to discard as untrue. This is the basis of your perception and this is the basis of your thoughts. Since your beliefs define your perception, your beliefs will define how you view yourself and how you interact with your surroundings.

The results of your thoughts work by creating more thoughts of the same in your mind and subsequently causing your choices and actions to mirror the types of thoughts that you currently have. If you believe that a life of abundance is not possible, then that is exactly what you will achieve; a life of abundance that is not possible for you. To believe in a life of abundance that is possible for you denotes that you must step beyond the normal classifications and limitations that you have set or accepted for yourself and the limitations that you have accepted from others.

Your core beliefs will create and perpetuate the thoughts that you have of yourself, whether these thoughts are good or bad. For example, if you believe that you will never have enough money to pay your bills, then that is exactly what you will produce; an experience where it seems as though you will never have enough money to pay your bills. On the other hand, if you believe that you will achieve a life of great abundance and you focus intently and consistently on these thoughts without allowing disempowering thoughts to dilute your efforts, then this is exactly what you will receive.

What is the current mental image that you have of yourself?

How can you change the vision of yourself in your mind in order to produce the desired outcome in your life?

Notes:

Date:_____

EVERY THOUGHT LEADS TO THE CREATION OF A SIMILAR THOUGHT

B y its very nature, the use of the mind during the thought process, conditions it and provides a mechanism for the creation of additional thoughts that are similar. Our state of mind is a derivative of the types of thoughts we have on a consistent basis, therefore, the beliefs and thoughts that produce a particular state of mind will continue to produce the same. There is always a synergy between the types of beliefs and thoughts we allow to flourish in our minds. Every thought we have or will ever have is a derivative of some previous thought or a combination thereof. In principle, our current thoughts have been inspired by our previous thoughts, which were developed based on OUR acceptance of certain beliefs of the past. Therefore, we must guard well the portals that allow disruptive beliefs and thoughts to enter our minds.

The thought generation process can be performed "manually", automatically or semi-automatically.

◘ A "manual" thought process takes place when we are fully in charge of the types of thoughts that are produced in our minds.

◘ An automatic process occurs when our thoughts, positive or negative, are generated seemingly without much effort on our part. These types of thoughts are typically synergistic in nature because the resulting thought is produced automatically from the previous thought without any "manual" intervention.

◘ A semi-automatic thought process is one where there may be dissimilar thoughts that are typically contradictory because they are inclusive of both elements of the "manual" and automatic thought process.

A contradiction may arise when thoughts that are produced automatically are simultaneously mixed with the more deliberate types of thoughts from the "manual" process. For example, disempowering thoughts may be automatically produced from an "unknown" subconscious belief while simultaneously empowering thoughts are deliberately introduced in an attempt to live a lifestyle of positive thinking. We typically migrate between the different types of thought processes based on our level of belief in what we are currently focusing on and the amount of mindfulness involved in the process.

Most of us either fall within the semi-automatic or fully automatic thought process at any given point in time. During the process of mindlessness, our thoughts are allowed to flow unchecked; consequently our negative thoughts will produce more and more negative thoughts in a seemingly automatic progression. Our thoughts are not just random bits of information that haphazardly "pop" into our minds, but are intrinsically based on what we believe. Therefore, if we believe that we will never have the type of life we desire, the types of thoughts that will permeate our minds will be based on this belief. These thoughts will not offer constructive criticism, solutions or ways to achieve the type of life that we desire, but will be entirely destructive, since the core belief is entirely destructive. A classic example is often seen when we are faced with what we perceive as a "problem". If our thoughts are based on the negative, we will intently focus on the "problem" itself and how it affects us emotionally. We will not recognize or we will choose to ignore the obvious solutions around us because we do not believe that we have an alternative choice in the matter.

There are always multiple options and opportunities

available. They become clearer as we calm our minds and allow ourselves to build upon empowering beliefs and thoughts. However, if no empowering thoughts are present, this indicates the absence of positive beliefs. We must take the initial step to intentionally produce the first positive belief, so that we can consequently build upon it with increasingly new and improved empowering thoughts. By realizing the importance of our current thoughts and the subsequent thoughts that they produce, we will mindfully monitor and correct any disempowering beliefs that creep into our minds. The old negative beliefs and thoughts of the past will still attempt to reveal themselves, but by consistently engaging in mindfulness, we can train our minds to eliminate the negative and grasp the positive.

What can you do to eliminate the proliferation of negative thought in your mind?

How can you change your beliefs in order to affect these thoughts?

Notes:

Date:_____

TO HAVE GOOD THOUGHTS YOU MUST STAY AWAY FROM BAD THOUGHTS

The simplicity and beauty of this statement is clearly understood by the mindful, however it creates much complexity in the mind of the non-believer. It sounds simple enough, however its execution is quite perplexing for many. Most do not realize that in order to have good thoughts, you have to have strong positive beliefs as the fundamental foundation.

How can you foster good thoughts when you are consistently thinking bad thoughts? How can you foster bad thoughts when you are consistently thinking good thoughts? If you were to examine the amount of times throughout the day that you engage in negative thinking, you probably would be surprised to find out that the amount of negative thoughts greatly supersede your positive thoughts. This undoubtedly accounts for the vast disarray in your life. The sheer volume of chaotic and frustrating thoughts far supersedes the amount of calm and empowering thoughts.

When you entertain disempowering thoughts, you leave no room in your mind for empowering thoughts. All thought, whether good or bad, is self-replicating in nature. The more of a particular type of thought you focus on, the more of the same is produced through self-generation. Since each thought requires more of the same in order to perpetuate its survival, more is automatically produced. Therefore, once you begin to deliberately introduce and subsequently focus on either positive or negative thoughts in your mind, your current beliefs will be altered as a result of this experience and thus they will change to justify the new thoughts and perceptions.

When your mind is filled with negativity such as disbelief, fear and frustration, you leave no room for positive thoughts to grow and flourish. Likewise, when your mind is filled with empowering thoughts, it leaves no room for disempowering thoughts to grow and flourish. Empowering thoughts create an environment and a breeding ground for more empowering thoughts, with positive results. Conversely, disempowering thoughts create an environment and a breeding ground for more disempowering thoughts, with negative results. Anytime you have empowering thoughts and subsequently introduce disempowering thoughts into your mind, you are creating a breeding ground for these disempowering thoughts to grow. These disempowering thoughts possess the potential to eventually overrun your available empowering thoughts and alter the results of your life in a negative way.

When you entertain empowering thoughts but do not possess true belief in your ability to achieve a life according to your desires, you are still creating an environment for disempowering thoughts such as disbelief to flourish. Any element of disbelief will cause negativity to begin to sprout like weeds in your mental garden. How can you maintain a positive momentum towards your goal when you do not actually and continuously believe that you will reach your goal? In order for you to reach your goal, you must believe 110%, 110% of the time. Any time disbelief is fostered, even for a second, it opens up the potential injection of disempowering thoughts and the negative consequences it brings.

Good thoughts in its purest form will trigger more of the same. The more positive and uplifting thoughts you possess, the more positive and uplifting thoughts you will continue to produce and possess. In this scenario, you are decreasing the room available for negativity and constructing additional rooms to house your positivity. However, when you disbelieve for any period of time, you are constructing additional rooms for disempowering thoughts to enter and occupy your mind while simultaneously decreasing the room available for empowering thoughts. With this action, you are diluting your empowering beliefs and affirmations in yourself and your ability to achieve your goal.

In order to maintain positive momentum in your life, you must resolve to refrain from any type of disempowering beliefs or interaction that produces negativity as a byproduct. When you are frustrated, filled with fear or possess chaotic thoughts, you must seek ways to eliminate these thoughts as quickly as possible. For example, if you desire to avoid being mugged, you would stay away from areas where mugging is prominent. Likewise, if you desire to have continuous positivity flowing into your life, you must make a continuous effort to eliminate the disempowering beliefs and thoughts. If you value the direction of your life, you must value the importance of having empowering beliefs and thoughts at all times.

There is an inverse relationship between positive and negative thoughts; an increase in one leads to a decrease in the other. Positive thoughts will not create negative thoughts and negative thoughts will not create positive thoughts. To do so would be a direct violation of either one's ability to exist. Therefore, if you relish the idea of having positive experiences in your life, you would savor the idea of maintaining positive beliefs and thoughts in your mind; the result of which is an increased production of the same.

You may believe that it is difficult or impossible to eliminate the negative thoughts from your mind; however, since you created and allowed the negative thoughts to proliferate in your mind, they can be ONLY destroyed by you. The negativity may have reached the point of habituation, but similar to the method used to break any other habit, you must introduce positive replacement beliefs and thoughts continuously in your mind until they too become habitual.

Do you consistently have negative thoughts in your mind?

Do you recognize the importance of constantly maintaining positive thoughts in your mind?

Notes:

Date:_____

WHEN YOU ARE HARD ON YOURSELF, YOU MAKE IT HARDER FOR YOURSELF

S elf-defeating beliefs and thoughts not only increase the mental stress being applied to you but they promote continued disbelief in your ability to eventually arrive at your goal. When you disbelieve that you will arrive at your goal, this disbelief will cause you to think and act in ways that are out of balance with the thoughts and actions required to reach your goal. You greatly decrease your chances of success by inflicting yourself with unnecessary turmoil; you are doing yourself a great disservice.

There are many things in life that you have to consider; deliberately making it hard on yourself must not be one of them. The very act of engaging in self-defeating beliefs and thoughts is by its very nature self-defeating. Since these beliefs and thoughts will only bring about more of the same types of thoughts, you are actually initiating an internal war within yourself that will slowly or rapidly destroy you depending on the frequency and magnitude of these self-defeating thoughts and actions. If your intention is to live a life of fulfillment, any belief, thought or action that is either physically or mentally destructive must be eliminated.

Often times it seems as though self-defeating thoughts are so easy to produce. Anytime you attempt to think thoughts that are contrary to these self-defeating thoughts, an internal battle ensues and if you are like most people, these self-defeating thoughts often win. Self-defeating thoughts typically overcome empowering thoughts due to a greater belief in the inability to succeed rather than the ability to succeed.

The frequency and magnitude of these thoughts are all based on what you believe. Before you can even begin to alter the type, frequency and magnitude of your thoughts, you must understand which types of beliefs form the basis of your core beliefs. Whenever you attempt to change the elements of your thoughts without first understanding your core beliefs, you will quickly find out that you are fighting a losing battle. Your attempts at thinking positively are simply a temporary fix and are masking the negative traits that are inherent in your belief system. The sting of your limiting core beliefs will rear its ugly head once again through the production of disempowering thoughts in the future. Therefore, a lifestyle of positive thinking without first addressing your underlying disempowering beliefs does not work.

A simple way to define your core beliefs is to travel back through time in your mind to locate the originating circumstances surrounding these beliefs. You can then dispute the validity of these beliefs. In most, if not all cases, you may find that the circumstances surrounding your core beliefs were simply your acceptance of the unfounded beliefs of another. This resulted in the creation of your belief in your inability to succeed which only served to make it harder on you.

Remember:

◙ No one can devalue you without your consent.

◙ No one can make it harder on you without you first making it harder on yourself by your very thoughts of yourself.

◙ When you are hard on yourself, this action only serves to allow others to continue the process which you have already started.

Whenever you have thoughts of non-deserving or not being good enough, the end result will never be good. These types of thoughts rip away at the very fabric of your being, causing you to question your very existence. These thoughts were generated from the negative beliefs that YOU accepted as a result of your past experiences and congregate to instill a value of you on yourself. Therefore, it is critical to examine and reexamine your current core beliefs anytime you begin to endorse self-defeating thoughts.

Do you sometimes think thoughts that make it hard on yourself?

Which beliefs are driving these thoughts?

Notes:

Date:_____

MOST OF US LIVE OUR LIVES PLANNING FOR NOTHING BUT THE OPPOSITE OF SUCCESS

I f you were to stop and ask an individual on the street if they are doing everything possible in life to succeed, most of them would probably utter a resounding yes. Most of them would probably admit to bouts of frustration and despair, but for the most part they believe that they are doing all that they possibly can in life. It is interesting to note however, the mechanistic view of "doing all that you possibly can in life". Doing all that you possibly can has multiple meanings depending on the perception of the viewer. It may indicate a tireless effort albeit based on a lack of mindfulness while another view may indicate an effort based on the perceived limitations in life. The first view defines an individual who may believe that they are relentlessly seeking success but their actions are contradictory to the receipt of the success while the later indicates an individual who may believe that life itself has imposed a set of limitations on their possibilities when in fact these limitations are self-created. However, both still indicate the presence of a limiting set of beliefs.

Anytime you perceive that you are doing all that you can do, you are imposing limitations on your life. Ironically this is contrary to the common belief of the masses because they view the limitations in life as merely an element of protection from a perceived future emotional discord. "Doing all that you can do" typically denotes a maximum potential based on a self-created limitation; a maximum potential based on an accepted limitation from external sources or a combination of both. However, one must never agree to the temptation of accepting their current situation as immutable and unchanging. In a world filled with possibilities, there are always avenues for improvement and fulfillment. Even though they may not be currently visible does not preclude the fact that they still exist. A change in perception and focus will provide a revelation of what is already available.

Many people allow themselves to become frustrated when the outcome of their lives is not in line with what they desire. Unfortunately, they do not realize that it is their beliefs, thoughts, choices and actions that are actually creating their experiences in life. But this common misconception runs deep throughout our society since most individuals are continually planning for the opposite of success just by the types of beliefs, thoughts and actions they produce on a continuous basis. How can you obtain success in your life when you do not believe that you will have success in your life? How can you obtain true fulfillment in your life when you do not believe that it is possible and you are deserving of this life of fulfillment? How can you obtain success in life when your beliefs, thoughts and actions are directing you away from success? True success and true fulfillment in life comes as a result of a prescribed vision of success in your mind, a belief in this vision that brings this vision to life and a committed focus on your thoughts and your actions through mindfulness to ensure that you are consistently in harmony with what is required to transform your vision into a reality. This is the only way that you can effectively plan your life for success. To do otherwise is an automatic plan for the opposite of success.

When you have contradictory thoughts about your life of success, you are ultimately planning your life for nothing but the opposite of success. Whatever you absolutely believe in your mind is exactly what you will achieve in your life. The limitations set forth by yourself and others will only serve as a hindrance and a stumbling block in your journey towards success. Anytime we believe and accept these limiting thoughts are "normal", we are planning for the opposite of success. Success is not about having limited thoughts or limitation of thought, but it is all about having thoughts that are limitless. The limitlessness of our beliefs, thoughts and perception actually define the level of commitment and dedication to persevere regardless of what is occurring in the world around us. When we believe in our ability to achieve what we desire and we continually focus on what we desire, we are constructing our world based on what we believe. It is extremely important that we remain mindful of our beliefs, thoughts and actions to ensure that we are constantly planning for success and not constantly planning for the opposite of success through our thoughts of disbelief.

Are you planning for success or the opposite of success?

How can you monitor your beliefs, thoughts and actions to ensure that they are based on the attainment of success?

Notes:

Date:_____

YOUR FUTURE IS BASED ON THE THOUGHTS YOU ARE THINKING IN THE PRESENT

Your present is a stepping stone to your tomorrow. As you sit and read this book, you are investing in your future. You are seeking the answers to the great question, "How can I improve my life?" Up to this point, the answer to this question may have eluded you. However, your quest for enlightenment still continues because of a void in your soul. You must, however, be grateful while simultaneously expanding your desire to fill the void in your life! It is through this conceptualized method of thinking, i.e., a process that involves the use of mindfulness to compare your beliefs, thoughts and actions relative to the creation of the results in your life, that the answers will eventually be revealed. I believe that if the notion of conceptual thinking is instilled, the world would be a better place. Unfortunately, the temptations of instant gratification, which are mentally and physically restrictive, negate the possibility of any type of inherent empowerment.

The present was once the future of your past.

All of the beliefs, thoughts and experiences of the past have shaped and molded the present, which will eventually become the past of your future. But unlike your past, you will be in a much better position to positively affect your future because of an understanding of how your present affects it. Every day of your life must be viewed as a building block for the foundation of your positive future. Therefore, you will value each and every experience, taking none for granted as you disallow the destructive thoughts of the past from festering and growing in your mind, causing disruption to the construction of your future positive foundation. Your belief in yourself and abilities must be intentionally increased in order to bring about the future that you desire.

Each and every present thought is a building block for the thoughts and actions of tomorrow. One thought leads to the creation of another similar thought, which eventually leads to the creation of an action based on the thought. When you disregard your current thoughts, you are literally disregarding your future. Likewise, when you place limitations on your current thoughts, you are in essence placing limitations on your future.

Oftentimes, we fail to analyze our current thoughts for clues on how they can be altered to promote our lives, but rather choose to analyze them based on how they affect our desire for instant gratification. If our emotions are mildly affected, we typically disregard the thought and its origin. We tend to only begin to consider our thoughts when our emotions are drastically affected by the circumstances around us; however, in the majority of cases, the relationship between our thoughts and our surroundings go unnoticed. However, even if our emotions are not seemingly materially affected, we must continue to maintain a fix on the direction of our thoughts. Even a small negative thought, deeply submerged in the hidden regions of our mind, can blossom into something colossal. The effect of this will be ultimately reflected in the results of our future.

Just like an individual who is planning for their retirement would begin to prepare well in advance to ensure their continued comfort, we too must begin to prepare well in advance to ensure a future that is not filled with discomfort. This preparation includes steadily focusing on maintaining the correct present beliefs and thoughts, regardless of our destructive emotional cravings. Please note that emotions are a valuable asset; however, the emotional cravings for instant gratification can be destructive and counterproductive. Much care must be given to the mindfulness of our thoughts and emotions as they relate to the attainment of the future we desire.

If we continue to nurture our microscopic negative thoughts, we should not be surprised when these thoughts multiply and deliver a devastating blow to our future. After all, continued nurturing and reinforcement serves as an enabler. On the other hand, if we continue to nurture our positive thoughts, we are enabling and positioning ourselves for a fulfilling future. Remember, a realization of what we desire comes as a result of a continuous monitoring and maintenance of our present beliefs, thoughts and actions to produce the desired outcome in the future.

What are your present thoughts about your life in the future?

_____

_____

How have these present thoughts been affected by your past beliefs?

_____

_____

Notes:

_____

_____

_____

_____

_____

_____

Date:_____

OTHER'S THOUGHTS ABOUT YOU ARE NOT YOUR THOUGHTS ABOUT YOU

E ach individual possesses the internal mechanism of belief, which is used to create their lives the way they "see" it in their minds. Each of us will obviously have very different past, present and future experiences because each of us possess a different set of core beliefs. Through our daily interactions with friends, family and peers, we sometimes have a tendency to "forget" or put aside our own set of beliefs and adopt the beliefs we perceive are being requested by others. In this case, our desire for acceptance overrules our desire for enlightenment and as such we adopt the limitations set forth by others.

Have you ever noticed how seemingly similar minded people automatically flock together during social events? The same patterns have transpired since we were young; popular people, nerds and "weirdoes" all tend to automatically create their own micro-society based on their perceived type of commonality. It is as though all autonomous thought and behavior is lost. The micro-society behaves as one single unit; the thoughts of the group become the thoughts of each of the members as each member automatically adopts the thoughts and behaviors set forth by the group. This classic example exemplifies the process whereby we consciously and subconsciously adopt the beliefs, thoughts and actions proposed by others.

However, when we relinquish our positively empowering beliefs about ourselves and replace them with the limiting beliefs and thoughts proposed by others, we are allowing their accepted limitations to become our life's limitations. However, even at this point we are still in control of our lives because a choice to live a life of limitation is still a choice.

The empowering thoughts we have of ourselves are based on the positive vision we have created in our minds. Therefore, why would we allow this vision to be altered by the limiting beliefs and perceptions of others? But here again, it all relates to the level of belief that we have in ourselves. When we have defined who we are and will become in our minds and continue to believe with commitment in this vision, any contradictory thought or action of another will not faze us because we "know" that it will not affect our quest for a life of success and fulfillment. We will be confident in our beliefs of who we are due to the awareness that it is OUR beliefs and not the beliefs of others that define who we are and will become.

Of course, there are certain instances where the beliefs of others can be added to our own. This can occur in the case where the beliefs of others are not limiting, but are empowering. However, our minds must be open to the acceptance of beliefs that are beyond the scope of our own. For example, if you were contemplating opening a new business and you were offered good advice from a "successful" business veteran, then by all means their beliefs may inevitably alter your beliefs. However, before we consider adopting the beliefs of others, we have to consider whether these newly proposed beliefs will limit or expand our current beliefs based on the intentions of our goal. If the beliefs are limiting, they must be rejected. On the other hand, if the beliefs are enlightening, they must be considered. Remember, any belief that acts as an enabler will bring us closer to our desired goal and the eventual receipt of our goal.

There must never be an automatic adoption of the beliefs of

another without careful consideration of the positive or negative effects they will have on our lives. The beliefs of another may be limiting based on the fears and frustrations of that individual. In Principle, when we adopt the limiting beliefs of others, we are also adopting their fears and frustrations. A desire for acceptance is never a good reason to sacrifice the effort made to accelerate our lives.

Do you typically change your beliefs, thoughts and actions depending on those with whom you are associated?

If so, how does this chameleon-like lifestyle affect your ability to receive your specific desires?

Notes:

Date:_____

CHAPTER 32

WHAT YOU DESIRE CANNOT BE OBTAINED BY FOCUSING ON THE OPPOSITE OF WHAT YOU DESIRE

Conflicting thoughts and imagery are prevalent in the way we conduct our lives. This is perhaps the main reason most of us are bombarded with the undesirable situations in our lives. We may have specific desires and goals in life, but the thoughts that we foster on a continued basis are literally causing us to choose actions that are leading us away from our desires. The vision of our life that we have in our minds will always be contradictory to our desires when our thoughts produce actions that lead us away from our desires. Unfortunately, these actions are commonly concealed within the habitual behaviors we classify as "normal". Typically, a "normal" action does not initiate a warning sign and thus we continue to perpetuate these destructive actions, unaware that they are misclassified as "normal".

Our opposing or contradictory thoughts often appear in the form of "little voices" in our minds that constantly attempt to interject disbelief in our ability to attain what we desire. These "little voices" of disbelief are based on our predefined limitations adopted from past experiences or the limiting beliefs accepted from others. For example, if there is a desire to live in a large home, we must not have limiting thoughts of lack related to our inability to live in a large home. Likewise, if there is a desire to drive a fancy car, we certainly must not allow our focus of what we believe is possible to be entirely on a car that is the opposite of what we desire. These opposing thoughts, whether conscious or subconscious, offer direct opposition and resistance to our ability to attain what we desire.

When mindfulness is not a part of our daily diet, the resistance in our lives that occurs both on a conscious and subconscious level is indiscernible. In both instances, we are unaware of its presence and therefore unaware of the correlation it has on our chosen course of action. Most of us not only subconsciously think in contradiction, but we also consciously think in contradiction anytime we choose to focus on the opposite of what we desire. When we have subconscious opposition, its presence is typically much more difficult to identify, however, both types of opposition will leave scars on our lives. Through the process of recapitulation (Refer to Appendix III), we can identify the limiting beliefs that are creating our conscious and subconscious opposition.

Opposing thoughts always emanate from the direction of our belief. For example, a desire to achieve success, coupled with a belief in our disbelief in our ability to achieve this success will produce opposing and contradictory thoughts. This disbelief can originate from our past experiences as well as the accepted beliefs from others with whom we are associated. This will undoubtedly cause the creation of the belief that the way things are is the way they should be because they have always been that way. "If our parents, friends and peers were unsuccessful at attaining their desires, why should we try?" is a common mantra believed by many. However, the reason our parents, friends and peers may not have been successful at achieving their desires can be traced back to THEIR set of limiting beliefs. If we decide to adopt the same limiting beliefs that have produced the same limiting outcome, our lives too will be limiting based on a decision to remain within the confines of these limitations. However, when we decide to revamp this outmoded method of thinking by broadening our horizons, the result of our lives will also be broadened.

It is extremely important to eliminate any semblance of doubt from our minds so that we can focus intently on obtaining what we desire through the disallowance of any self-defeating thoughts from infiltrating our minds. When our minds are calm, we are better able to manage the myriad of thoughts that float in and out of our minds. Additionally, we are better able to identify the core beliefs that are actually producing our conflicting thoughts. When we begin to challenge our core beliefs and alter them for the better, we are literally challenging our old ways of thinking and altering them for the better. No longer do we have to think in opposition to what we desire. We will be empowered to think in harmony with our desires.

What "little voices" do you hear on a daily basis that incites disbelief in your mind?

How do these voices affect your level of belief and commitment?

Notes:

Date:_____

THE POWER OF YOUR LIFE COMES FROM THE POWER OF YOUR THOUGHTS

The human mind is a powerhouse full of potential. However, this potential is literally a double-edged sword; producing positive power or negative power depending on the choice of the individual wielding the power. The intensity of this power in either direction varies from individual to individual depending on what the individual believes is possible or impossible. Thus, an individual who focuses on negativity grants great power to the manifestation of negative outcomes in their life, while simultaneously granting limited power to the creation of positivity in their life. Each of us exhibit some form of power in our lives every time we make decisions that affect our lives for the good or bad.

Unfortunately, the true power of choice is not understood by most; otherwise, more thought would be given to the potential consequences prior to engaging in the action. The ability to choose and the choices that are formulated through the use of this ability, are the basis of human existence and control every aspect of life, ranging from past, present and future experiences. Thoughts that are extremely powerful produce choices that are extremely powerful, which invariably result in a life that is extremely powerful and rewarding. However, if chaotic and unfocused thoughts are allowed to germinate, the resulting choices will become chaotic and unfocused, creating a life that will follow suit.

Everything in life revolves around the amount of power that is emitted from thought. Mindfulness promotes an increase in the level of thought filled with awareness, determination and focus. Mindfulness further promotes an awareness of thought and emotion, ensuring that all thought is continually being emitted at a powerful level that will only create good experiences in life. Anything below this level will only seek to dilute the power potential and cause a diversion away from the prime objective. Mindlessness, on the other hand, is commensurate to thought that is unfocused and thus promotes complacency, stagnation, frustration and complaining; all of which are undesired results.

Any time negativity and disbelief are allowed to creep into the mind, it WILL dilute the intense mental positive power potential. Consequently, each positive thought will become progressively weaker with each passing moment, while each negative thought will become progressively stronger. Negative thoughts are parasitic in nature and actively attach to the most powerful positive thoughts with the intention of destroying them. Therefore, the mental environment must be cleansed regularly through a daily practice of meditation (Refer to Appendix V). A regular meditation regiment will quiet the mind and cleanse the parasitic elements that are actively destroying and disrupting your life. The ability to harness the true power of positive thought will come as a result of continuous practice and emersion. The initial stages may appear to be daunting, however, through commitment and a decision to persevere and focus on the benefits of achieving a life filled with positive power, maximization of the true positive power potential will be attained.

The current negative thoughts have not been developed overnight, but have been constructed over time as a result of past experiences. Please note that any movement that is in opposition to the already rooted dogma will inherently bring resistance. However, this resistance can be overcome, but the speed at which it is developed is based solely on the intensity of what is desired. A car cannot safely turn 180 degrees when the brakes are abruptly depressed. The momentum must be decreased before it is safe to make a change in direction. Likewise, if the negative power of thought is at full throttle, a decrease in its momentum through mindfulness will enable a change in direction towards positive thought.

I encourage you to seek to make changes in your thought pattern, by focusing exclusively on empowering beliefs and thoughts, which will increase as momentum increases in the opposite direction.

Do you desire to have powerful positive thoughts?

Are you fully committed to affecting a change in your life?

Notes:

Date:_____

A ROAD IS ONLY MADE ROUGH BY THE POTHOLES YOU PLACE IN IT

There are some roads that contain potholes while others do not. The ones with the potholes are obviously much more difficult to travel than the ones without potholes. If you had a choice of traveling along a road without potholes versus traveling along a road with potholes, I am sure you would elect to travel the road without potholes due to its ease of travel.

A pothole is anything that offers resistance to the receipt of your desires. Your limiting beliefs, thoughts of non-deserving and the retention of the negativity of your past experiences are all classic examples of the potholes you produce that create resistance in your life. Any time you allow disempowering thoughts to infiltrate your mind or allow disbelief, non-deserving or poverty consciousness to alter your thoughts and your actions, you are placing potholes in the road to your life of fulfillment and abundance. This is one of the great ironies of life because if you were to step back and think about how your beliefs, thoughts and actions are contributing to the production of potholes in your life, you would not produce the potholes that impede your life.

You can also allow the potholes of life to be inserted by others through your acceptance of their imposing limiting beliefs. But your acceptance of these limiting beliefs is actually the result of your own disbelief in your ability to achieve your goal. Remember that the road that you have chosen to travel is based on your beliefs as well as the beliefs you accept from outside sources. When you allow these external sources to influence your beliefs, thoughts and perceptions in a negative way, you are allowing these forces to control and dictate the creation of your path in life.

Since everything is based on your perception, a "problem" isn't necessarily a "problem" if you choose to change your perception of it. However, when you believe that a life without potholes is either falsely euphoric or unrealistic, aren't you essentially creating potholes where there were none?

Unfortunately, many of us have been preprogrammed through social and experiential conditioning to disregard how our beliefs, thoughts and perceptions are literally offering resistance to our ability to achieve our desires through the creation of potholes in our life. We typically believe that there is something amiss if the road is "too smooth" since we are commonly under the impression that a "normal" and realistic life is based on a road which contains at least a few potholes. But why is it so difficult to perceive a life without potholes? The common misconception is that a life without "problems" is a false sense of euphoria.

What potholes are you creating in your road to success?

Which beliefs are triggering the creation of these potholes?

Notes:

Date:_____

IF YOU THINK IN THE PAST YOU WILL REMAIN IN THE PAST

Thinking and retaining the old ideologies of the past will cause your thoughts and actions to be identical to those of the past. If your beliefs, thoughts and actions are identical to those of the past, you can also expect your experiences to be identical or have a close resemblance to those of the past. Since your experiences are produced as a result of your beliefs, thoughts and actions, it implies that if your experiences are identical or virtually identical to the experiences of the past. Therefore, your beliefs, thoughts and actions must also be identical or virtually identical to those of the past.

"Self-analysis" is perhaps an uncomfortable word that most people try to avoid. But if performed objectively, it will undoubtedly reveal "truths" about your personality that may be unpleasant and unbearable to accept. However, the true purpose of self-analysis must be the identification of self-defeating destructive patterns of behavior and not the characterization of your deficiencies. When taken in its true form, self-analysis must actually be highly embraced, because it is through this process that you are able to identify your self-defeating and destructive patterns of behavior. How can you improve and promote your physical and mental well-being if you are not willing to ascertain the destructive behaviors that are creating the undesired experiences in your live?

When you complain and make excuses about your situation, you are not allocating the time to examine which internal and external forces are actually driving your current experiences. If you were to reflect on your past patterns of thoughts and actions, you will be able to undoubtedly identify specifically associated experiences. There is always a specific consequence produced as a result of your beliefs, thoughts and actions. However, it is up to you to become mindful in order to recognize the patterns that are producing these undesired results. However, to partake of the benefits of this revelation requires a bit of self-analysis.

Since you are the driving force behind your past, present and future experiences, what is the point of complaining? You complain when you feel vulnerable in your current situation; but think about it, you are in fact the one who actually created the situation. When you continue to adhere to your old ways of thinking, you continue to remain in the past and will eventually succumb to the exact experiences you had in the past. If you desire a change in your life in the present, there must be a change in your beliefs and your thinking in order to produce the necessary changes in your present actions. A change in your old perspective as a result of a change in your past core beliefs will provide the necessary changes you desire in your life.

Unfortunately, many of us do not realize that it is through our believing, thinking and action processes that we are literally creating our present experiences and also building upon our past and present experiences to produce our future experiences.

Are your present experiences identical or similar to those of the past?

Are you holding on to the old ideologies and limitations of the past?

Notes:

Date:_____

THINKING WITHIN A LIMITED CONFINE FURTHER LIMITS THE CONFINEMENT TO WHICH YOU ARE LIMITED

I magine that you are living in a 4000 sq. ft. home and one day decided to move into a 700 sq. ft. home. I am sure that the confinement of the 700 sq. ft. home would have major implications on what you are able to do and how you are able to enjoy your life. By making such a move, you have just limited your boundaries because the smaller home obviously cannot accommodate the type of lifestyle to which you have grown accustomed. Likewise, if you intentionally limit your thinking from the possibilities of the 4000 sq. ft. home to the confines of the 700 sq. ft. home, you cannot experience the luxury and the splendor offered by the 4000 sq. ft. home. Figuratively, you are missing out on all of the opportunities that the greater thinking area has to offer.

But why would someone desire to deliberately move from a 4000 sq. ft. home to a 700 sq. ft. home you may ask or even more notably, why would someone want to move into a 700 sq. ft. home when a 4000 sq. ft. home is easily available to them? Actually, it all relates to the types of beliefs that the individual has and also the strength of these beliefs. Obviously, if someone chooses to elect the limitations of the smaller home over the abundant lifestyle of the larger home, they either do not believe that they can achieve an abundant lifestyle or they do not feel as though they deserve a life of abundance. Whatever the case, they do not realize that whatever they can think of, if they truly believe and are committed to this belief, they can achieve!

Frustration, non-deserving and not being good enough are elements that are a major cause of a life of limitation. These types of thoughts will first destroy the vision of the foundation of the 4000 sq. ft. home in your mind and instead create a new foundation based on 700 sq. ft. These self-imposed limitations will consequently reconstruct your life based on the limitations of your self-imposed limited blueprint. These limitations will solidify your previous limiting beliefs which in turn will become your reality in your "real" world that is overflowing with frustration and limitation. However, your beliefs and thoughts are under your control and can be changed by you. These disempowering and limiting beliefs and thoughts must be eliminated from your mind because they only serve to act as blinders that prohibit you from recognizing solutions or opportunities for a better life.

When you believe that your life will always be filled with limitations, the thoughts that are produced as a result will be based on a limited point of view. This represents a deliberate placement into a life of limited confinement. As a result of this limited point of view, you will forgo the opportunity to look beyond the current limits that you have set for yourself whether consciously or subconsciously; intentionally or unintentionally. Either way, these limitations will be set in place because of what you believe and will further restrict the confines to which you have deliberately placed yourself. Any time your beliefs restrict you to a limited space, there is no way to move beyond the limitations of this space unless you believe that it is possible for you to do so and you are willing to expand your sphere of belief.

When you are in the confines of your own limitations, anything beyond these confines is perceived as impossible or non-existent. You are only cognizant of the limitations of your own confines because this is what you have chosen to accept. This is the only thing that you believe is possible and attainable. The belief and possibility matrix (Refer to Appendix IV) can help you to challenge your current set of limiting beliefs by concluding that beliefs beyond your current sphere of association abundantly exist. You can accomplish much more than you originally believed; you simply have to intentionally believe that it is possible and the answers will come.

What are your current belief confines?

How can you move beyond your current limitations?

Notes:

Date:_____

MASTERY OF CONTROLLING YOUR THOUGHTS COMES WHEN YOU LOSE THE CONTROL OF YOUR LIMITATIONS

C ontrolled intentional thought is the process of purging unwanted thoughts and replacing them with desired thoughts. As easy as this may sound, it is still a process because the unwanted thoughts have become habitual due to their continued usage over time. But in order to effectively initiate this process, you must first value it and the potential benefits it brings. If you perceive that the effort required supersedes the applicable benefits even though you believe in the benefits, you will not engage in this process. But when you perceive that the benefits supersede the effort required and there is belief in the achievement of these benefits, there will be a high level of commitment to the success of the process.

One of the most important steps in this process is the awareness that your current thoughts are indeed negative and not simply just a normal and acceptable function of life. Any thought or inferences that place restrictions and limitations on your positive beliefs and positive actions are disempowering and detrimental. Unfortunately, these types of thoughts and inferences have become intertwined into the very fabric of our society and thus have been virtually concealed from recognition. Thus, what is actually restrictive and limiting has now become a "normal" way of life. The unenlightened individual makes use of these limiting beliefs without realizing their very presence. Through the process of domestication, we habitually nurture these negative limiting thoughts and rebel against those who think otherwise.

When you accept the preconceived notion that there is no other way available to you besides the limitation to which you have become accustomed, you are relying on the limitations set forth internally and externally. Anytime you feel trapped in your life, you are accepting the limitations of your limiting thoughts. These negative limiting thoughts force you to believe that you will never succeed in your life because you do not have a choice. Ironically you choose to settle with "what life has dealt you" without realizing that settling is actually the absolute acceptance of that which you have created. This assumption that your choices are limited is so far from the truth.

Mastering our thoughts consists of the awareness that our thoughts are limited in the first place. It is simply our continued belief and perception that our lives are limited and will always continue to be limited that places further limitations on an already limited state of mind. When we lose the control that our limiting beliefs have over us, we enter a realm that is not based on the frustration of our lives unfulfilled, but one that is based on mindfulness. Our limiting beliefs have created the mechanistic view that we have no other alternatives in our physical world or in our mental world as well.

By taking the time to analyze our thoughts and emotions, we can identify the beliefs that are limiting our lives and begin to take steps to eradicate them from our "mental vocabulary". Beliefs that are illogical and have no basis must be replaced with specialized beliefs that are specifically designed for the attainment of our goals. A mastery of injecting our minds with these specialized beliefs and thoughts will prove to maintain our path and momentum towards our goal.

What types of limiting thoughts do you currently have?

_____

_____

How can you change your beliefs so that you can lose the control that your limiting beliefs have over you?

_____

_____

Notes:

_____

_____

_____

_____

_____

_____

Date:_____

OUR THOUGHTS ARE THE PRIMARY CAUSE OF EVERYTHING WRONG IN OUR LIVES

E verything you think, say or do have an origin related to your past and present beliefs and perceptions. These beliefs and perceptions have a direct and indirect impact on your current and future actions, since they also directly impact your current and future thoughts. If your thoughts are balanced and exist in harmony with the intentions of your goal, you will achieve your goals. However, if your thoughts are not aligned correctly with the intentions of your goal, your actions will propel you away from your goal.

The alignment of your thoughts represents thoughts that are free of chaos and frustration. Unlike their counterparts which flow haphazardly, thoughts that are aligned and harmonious flow evenly and can be easily managed. Anytime there is the presence of a thought that is destructive to the attainment of your intentions, it must be eradicated immediately after the source of the negativity is determined. If you immediately attempt to eradicate the thought without having a clear understanding of the dynamics of the thought, you will simply be temporarily removing the symptom and not the root cause. The thought will emerge again, oftentimes unexpectedly, to strike at the very heart of your desires, with the intention of disrupting your balanced and harmonious thoughts.

The major challenge that most of us face is the continued mindfulness of our thoughts. This process must occur on a conscious and a subconscious level and can only be obtained through a continuous emersion until it too becomes habitual in the conscious and subconscious mind. To understand this process is to understand the importance of mindfulness. Our actions are a result of our thoughts…so you can imagine how detrimental incorrect thoughts can be. Once we become mindful of our thoughts we can actually alter the detrimental thoughts and resultantly circumvent the destructive actions that will only serve to divert us away from your goal. The process of mindfulness becomes increasingly easier when the underlying beliefs that drive our detrimental thoughts are altered. A belief based on your absolute success and a knowing based on this belief will produce thoughts that are in harmony with your intentions. Thus, more and more empowering thoughts are produced while simultaneously fewer and fewer counterproductive thoughts are produced.

Mindfulness denotes the awareness of the types of thoughts that are constructed as a result of your current beliefs. Mindfulness also implies a comparison between the thoughts required to achieve your goal and your current thoughts as they relate to the achievement of your goals. Mindfulness fundamentally envelopes the maintenance and periodic housekeeping process to alter or delete the destructive beliefs that have been amassed over time. This accumulation of beliefs generally develops from childbirth thus forming a solid foundation for the basis of your current beliefs.

Since our subconscious beliefs affect our conscious beliefs, we can utilize our conscious beliefs to define our subconscious beliefs through the process of recapitulation (Refer to Appendix III). Once these subconscious beliefs are defined, they can be altered or eradicated through the process of intentional belief (Refer to Appendix VI). You are able to verify the type of beliefs and thoughts you currently possess by validating the product of your actions. For example, when negative experiences plague your life, the first course of action must be to look within to establish how your beliefs, thoughts and actions are actually creating these negative experiences instead of attempting to deflect the blame onto someone or something. The results of our lives are negative because our beliefs, thoughts and actions are detrimental due to the presence of fear and frustration in our lives. Fear and frustration is present because of a fundamental absence of true belief.

Your thoughts are based on your conscious and subconscious beliefs; they are the primary cause of your subsequent actions and therefore the primary cause of the experiences in your life. Whatever end results you desire, correct thoughts are paramount to its achievement. As you continually practice monitoring your thoughts and adjusting both your beliefs and thoughts as needed, then and only then can you begin to receive what you desire.

How are your current thoughts affecting the consequences in your life?

Do you have the tendency to blame others for these consequences?

Notes:

Date:_____

WE AUTOMATICALLY THINK THE WORST BEFORE WE AUTOMATICALLY THINK THE BEST

I t is amazing how we tend to automatically gravitate towards the production of negatively charged reactions as opposed to embodying positively charged responses. Whenever the results in our lives appear to contradict our desires, we tend to automatically think the worst of the situation. Understandably, thoughts relative to our past experiences can perform as an emotional protective mechanism, but we should not allow our negative emotions to overshadow the prime directive. If we "win" emotionally, that is, satisfy our primal cravings through instant gratification, do we not loose characteristically?

A typical example of this comes in the form of a limiting statement such as "Do not get your hopes up too high" or "Your goals are too lofty." All of these are examples of what we have been socially conditioned to accept throughout the course of our lives. Sure, these statements are geared towards protecting us from "potential" emotion disappointments however; their adoption ultimately limits our future potential.

What we are able to achieve has been drastically limited based on our acceptance of these limiting statements and others similar to them. Yes, these statements appeal to our sense of security, but they produce long lasting and detrimental effects of limitation in our lives.

Automatically thinking in the negative will never yield a positive result.

The paramount impetus for automatically gravitating towards the negative is due to the presence of disbelief. It is amazing how the power of belief in our disbelief affects every aspect of our lives, but its effects typically go unnoticed by most. Unfortunately, we do not believe in the positive since we are too busy focusing on the negative and its associated disbelief. When we believe in the positive, we will automatically offer accolades to ourselves and to others. Ironically, any time someone automatically thinks for the best instead of the worst, they are frequently perceived as dreamers and are often scoffed and mimicked by others because of their pursuit for "apparently" lofty goals and ideas. These "dreamers" are also ridiculed because of their non-acceptance and non-compliance with the limitations set forth by the masses.

When we think of the worst as being highly probable, we are dooming our present and our future life of success. If we absolutely desire to achieve success, why would we assume that the worst is inevitable? The answer to this question rests simply in the following:

(A) We do not believe that we will achieve a life of success.

(B) We do not believe in our ability to achieve a life of success.

(C) We do not believe that we deserve a life of success.

(D) We do not believe that a life of success is actually possible for us.

Based on these disempowering perceptions, we will always continue to believe and think that we will not achieve and receive success in our lives. We are too busy "protecting" ourselves emotionally at the expense of our personal fulfillment. But isn't a life devoid of personal fulfillment a destructive blow to our emotional well-being? The amount of complaining and frustration within our lives is a testimony to this fact. Thus, a decision to automatically gravitate towards the negative as a savior for our emotions will actually reveal a demon in disguise.

Do you find yourself automatically gravitating towards the negative?

How is your current level of belief affecting this gravitational pull towards the negative?

Notes:

Date:_____

OUR THOUGHTS ARE LIKE WATER... THEY FOLLOW THE PATH OF LEAST RESISTANCE

A river flowing aimlessly certainly does not produce as much power as one that is controlled by a dam. The dam controls and regulates the flow of water which can be used to produce energy in a specific form; by harnessing the power potential of the water and allocating it to be used in a prescribed manner according to some specific guideline. If the river is allowed to flow haphazardly, there will be an overall reduction and dilution of its power potential. Without the dam, the water would flow along the path of least resistance and produce no real energy benefit. Thus, the river is unable to accomplish more than its undiluted form. This analogy, when compared to our thoughts, can produce an appreciation for the true essence of undiluted and subjugated thoughts and actions.

Our thoughts are like water flowing in a river. If allowed to flow aimlessly, no real positive energy is produced. There is literally an overall dilution of the power potential of thought and thus an overall dilution of the power potential of the mind. However, when we subjugate and regulate our thoughts like a dam controls and regulates the flow of water, we can harness the power potential of these controlled thoughts to produce our desired outcome. Our power potential become focused and concentrated thus we can accomplish much more than the diluted form.

When we allow our thoughts to flow unchecked and haphazardly, we are actually practicing mindlessness in its truest form. Within the constructs of our minds, we must not only allow thoughts to grow, but have specific thoughts which will produce specific actions required for the attainment of a specific goal. When our thoughts run aimlessly and unchecked, we begin to harbor traces of disempowering thoughts that flow in and out of our empowering thoughts. If allowed to grow unchecked, these disempowering thoughts can eventually dominate and overpower our empowering thoughts. Additionally, if our focus is allowed to flow aimlessly, we will not be able to produce the necessary power or initiative that will enable us to accomplish our goal. When we appropriate our focus to concentrating on the solution to a "problem" and not the "problem" itself, we are focusing our energy on a higher benefit; the recognition of a solution to the "problem". Conversely, when we misappropriate our focus to a concentration on the "problem" exclusively, we are diluting our creative energy potential; the results of which are always disastrous.

Our thoughts will always flow aimlessly and unchecked through the practice of mindlessness. These thoughts, by their very nature will elect to flow down the path of least resistance. Thoughts of limitation, non-deserving, not being good enough and even the negative energy from friends, family and peers will quickly permeate our minds and become a function of our daily routine. We must resist these types of thoughts so that our actions will always meet the requirements for us to arrive at our goal.

Are your thoughts flowing haphazardly or are they controlled?

Do you believe in the power potential of controlled thoughts and actions?

Notes:

Date:_____

FLOWING WATER CLEANS AND REFRESHES; STAGNANT WATER BREEDS DISEASE

The way you live your life can be compared to either a body of water that is constantly flowing or a body of water that is stagnant. When your life resembles flowing water, you possess a positive momentum and you are continuously and mindfully working your plan so that you can arrive at your goal. Conversely, when your life resembles stagnant water, you possess habitual thoughts and characteristics that are destructive and will continue to breed frustration and despair. When your entire focus is on the positive elements of life, you are more inclined to continue to focus on the positive elements of life.

Anytime you introduce or allow negativity to be introduced into your life, you weaken and diminish your current level of positive energy and replace it with negative energy. The more negative thought energy you introduce into your mind, the more negative thought energy will be produced. Likewise, the more positive thought energy you introduce into your mind, the more positive thought energy will be produced.

Your life is a direct reflection of the types of beliefs and thoughts you engross. Anytime you continue to follow the same old limited patterns of believing and thinking while expecting a different result, you are exhibiting traits of stagnant water. Likewise, when your focus is exclusively on the negative, you encourage the breeding of stagnant water. The results will naturally breed frustration, anxiety and fear into your life.

There are numerous ways of eliminating this negativity so that your life can begin to flow in a manner that revitalizes and reconditions. The first step in this alteration process involves a decision to improve your life and a commitment to this decision; otherwise all subsequent actions will be futile. When you make a decision to improve your life while possessing a high level of commitment to this decision of change, you can then examine your past and present beliefs and thoughts and compare them to the specific beliefs and thoughts that are required to obtain your objective. If they differ, you must make the necessary changes in order for your current beliefs and thoughts to be in harmony with those required to obtain your objective.

Positive energy always cleans and revitalizes your spirit because your focus is on the joy that you will experience when you achieve your desired results. During this process, you are literally fixated on the joy as though you have already achieved your desired results. However, when you offer any resistance to a life of abundance in the form of negativity and destructive behavioral patterns, you are offering resistance to the flow of positive energy into and through your life. The amount of resistance that you offer will depend on the level of belief you have in achieving your life of abundance. The greater the level of disbelief; the greater the resistance and the more stagnant your life becomes.

The disease of the mind (negative thinking) is its own ability to circumvent and destroy its power potential to create a life of abundance. Unfortunately, this disease, once introduced into the mind, will begin to spread exponentially and eventually commence an invasion of the mind. No longer will your life flow with positive energy, but the stagnancy of this negative energy will subjugate the mind and produce the ravaging effects of fear, frustration and despair.

You must not allow your mind to limit your mind! Intuitively, the process of true self-fulfillment must be embraced, since it is through this process that the mind, body and soul are able to benefit from enlightenment.

Is your life currently flowing or is it stagnant?

How can you remove the negative beliefs that are prohibiting and restricting the flow of your life?

Notes:

Date:_____

WHEN YOU ARE TOO BUSY FOCUSING ON THE NEGATIVE, THE POSITIVE WILL ELUDE YOU

We are often too busy focusing on the negative and how it affects us emotionally that we fail to see the positive in each situation.

If your current belief resonate a life that will continue to be filled with negativity, that is all you will "see"; your life filled with negativity, fear and frustration. You will continue to perceive only negativity around you even though positively abounds. It is through your beliefs that you select the filters that are used to add definition to your perception of the world within you and around you. These beliefs set the parameters in which your perception uses to define and categorize the world around you. How many times have you lost sight of something that was right in front of you because you were focused on something else?

Take for example, if you are looking for your favorite pen on a cluttered table, you may not see it because your focus is on the clutter and the associated frustration with the clutter instead of maintaining a focus on the search for the pen exclusively. Your focus on the clutter does not preclude the fact that the pen is right in front of you, even though you may not see it. However, the pen becomes more and more elusive as the level of frustration increases and your thoughts become increasingly chaotic because your frustration functions as a blinding veil. However, when you begin to calm your mind, your chaotic focus becomes increasingly focused. The blinding veil created by your frustration is lifted and the pen is revealed to you. It is important to note that the blinding veil created by your frustration does not signify that the pen was not available to you. It was already available to you regardless of your inability to see it. Additionally, if your frustration level continues to increase, the pen will continue to elude you. The same principle applies to your life of success and fulfillment.

When you focus on the negative aspects of life, you will not perceive the positive aspects that are right in front of you. The positivity of life will continue to be elusive. However, you will not perceive it until you first decide to calm the frustrating and destructive thoughts that are causing the misappropriation of your focus. I believe that the common analogy of turning over a cup when you are looking for something actually disrupts your current focus, causing you to have a shift in your focus from the frustration of what you are currently searching for, to the action of turning over the cup. Not only does it disrupt your current misappropriated focus, but it also gives you an opportunity to calm your mind and reduce the amount of frustration. When you turn over the cup, you actually believe that you will find what you are searching for; however, this belief is in calmness and not shrouded by frustration. Your focus is no longer on the frustration of your inability to locate the item, but is now calmly focused on finding the item.

Mindfulness is extremely important because it is through this exercise that you become aware of the direction of your focus. Additionally, it promotes the awareness of the consequences of your thoughts because you have previously experienced these thoughts and have observed their consequences in the past. In principle, when you are mindful of your thoughts, you will quickly seek to nurture those that are positive and eliminate those that are negative as soon as they arise.

You will not allow them to flourish and will not nurture them through continuous enablement.

Whatever we focus on will become the truth of what is "real" and also what is revealed to us. Naturally, if our every waking moment is spent in worry and fear concerning our present situation, our perception will automatically seek out each and every instance of frustration and fear in our lives in order to justify this perception and maintain it. Amazingly, even the elements of our lives that are positive will begin to be viewed as negative, since the purpose of our focus is to highlight only the negative. There is no way to perceive the positive when our beliefs, thoughts and actions are emphasizing and searching exclusively for the negative. Thus, our lives will continue to remain negative even though others around us are enjoying the positivity of the life they have chosen to perceive and accept.

Do you find yourself constantly focusing on the negative?

If so, how are your beliefs directing your thoughts in a negative direction?

Notes:

Date:_____

POSITIVE EMOTIONS BUILD UPON POSITIVE EMOTIONS

A small action, when allowed to perpetuate, carries with it the energy to produce an even greater action. Our decision to engage in negative or positive thinking based on our current beliefs is no different. A single belief, when harnessed and nurtured, has the potential to produce an idea that is virtually unstoppable. This gradual increase in the momentum of a single belief, thought or action has the potential to change the life of the individual generating the belief, thought or action as well as those around them. Once there is sufficient momentum, a belief, thought or an action will seemingly flow freely based on its ability to use its current momentum to further increase its momentum.

All thoughts, whether positive or negative, have the ability to use its current momentum to drastically increase its momentum. For example, a negative thought, when perpetuated and allowed to flow freely through our minds, will use its momentum for the production of more thoughts that are negative. Likewise, a positive thought, when perpetuated and allowed to flow freely, will use its momentum for the production of more thoughts that are positive. In summary, positive thoughts and emotions build upon positive thoughts and emotions whereas negative thoughts and emotions build upon negative thoughts and emotions.

Most of us either do not realize that we are engaging in habitually destructive habits or realize the importance of NOT engaging in any type of habitually destructive activity. Additionally, most of us do not realize that since negative emotions produce more negative emotions, then by its very nature, positive emotions will produce more positive emotions. Many people believe that having a few positive thoughts intertwined with massive amounts of negative thoughts constitute positivity. Still others believe that having lots of positive thoughts coupled with periodic bouts of prolonged negativity constitutes positivity. Unfortunately, this is not so.

In its purest form, positivity is the process of creating and maintaining the powerful thoughts that will help us arrive at our goal of fulfillment while analyzing and subsequently eliminating any negative thoughts before they become habitual. The caveat here is that before we can successfully eliminate our negative thoughts and create positive long lasting replacements, we MUST first examine our current beliefs and seek to eliminate our negative limiting beliefs and replace them with positive empowering beliefs. In Principle, anytime we analyze our negative thoughts, our intention must be to seek out the origin of these thoughts and change the related beliefs relative to our past experience so that our present and future thoughts are no longer plagued by the influences of the past. This change can be accomplished through a transformation in perception of our past experiences. No longer must they be viewed in a negative light; they must be viewed as stepping stones for the creation of a brighter tomorrow.

When we are continually mindful of our thoughts and emotions, we leave no room for negativity, because we are constantly analyzing our negative thoughts and replacing them with positive thoughts through a change in our system of beliefs. The more positive thoughts we add to our thought stream, the more momentum they will produce. As soon as we allow any negative thought to fester in our minds, we construct dams that restrict the free flow positive thoughts and hamper our positive momentum. These negative dams will only allow our negative thoughts to flow through our minds, thereby building even greater negative momentum. The positive thoughts will eventually be ostracized and banished from our minds in order to make room for the negativity.

Destroying the dams of negativity and ensuring that they are NOT reconstructed is an ongoing process of mindfulness that takes time to develop. However, the more we practice, the more proficient we will become. The most important part of the process is not the process itself, but the decision to engage in the process. Note that it is far easier to engage in negative thought patterns than it is to engage in positive thought patterns. But if we value our lives of fulfillment, we will consistently seek to engage in positive thought patterns while rejecting the negative thought patterns so often instilled though social and experiential conditioning.

Do you have more negative or positive thoughts?

How can you build upon your positive thoughts to increase your positive momentum in your life?

Notes:

Date:_____

WE DESIRE TO EXPERIENCE POSITIVITY, BUT WE ARE THE BIGGEST SOURCE OF NEGATIVITY

Would anyone deliberately invite negativity into his or her life while claiming to be on a quest for positivity? Ironically, many of us may claim that we are seeking positive experiences and disdain negative experiences, but our lives are often enveloped in negativity. The answer is quite simple. The negativity that we are constantly experiencing is emanating from and through us. Whenever we adhere to the negative beliefs of the past and allow them to construct our beliefs in the present, the negative beliefs of the past are increased exponentially because our focus knows nothing more than negativity. Instead of complaining about "what life has dealt us", we must actually look within ourselves to locate the source of the negative force that is creating our current situation. Since our external experiences are predicated on our internal experiences, our negative external experiences must be as a result of our negative internal experiences.

The results of our lives are either directly or indirectly within our control. We may not have direct control over the peripheral elements such as the unexpected traffic jam or the car failing to start, but we can however choose how we will respond to these situations so that they positively affect our intentions and emotions. We can also choose how we will respond to the elements in our lives that we do have direct control over. The responses we choose will directly and indirectly determine the outcome and subsequently create a positive or negative experience. For example, when we are stuck in an unexpected traffic jam with the possibility of being late for work, the initial reaction is typically based on frustration and fear. This frustration and fear is derived from a belief that the end result will NOT be according to our desires. The frustration produced can lead to a lack of mindfulness which potentially can result in an accident. An alternative response could be to listen to a self-help CD. Yes, we may not be able to directly subjugate the flow of traffic, but we can directly control our response to it as it relates to achieving our objective.

When we believe and know that the outcome will be according to our desires, we eliminate the fear and frustration, thus making room for positivity in our lives. On the other hand, whenever we become frustrated, we invite additional negative energy into our lives. We are the sole authors of the negative thoughts and frustrations that run rampantly through our minds. Frustration used as measurable feedback is a mechanism in which the current situation is compared to the desired situation and the deficiency is analyzed to determine how your current beliefs, thoughts and actions are contributing to its creation of this deficiency. However, frustration that is not used as measurable feedback to help improve our lives will automatically produce negativity.

Can you count the number of times during the day that you became frustrated? Each of these instances, no matter how seemingly trivial, is a seed for an even bigger bout of frustration. It is also important to note that frustration is not only produced from inner turmoil, but also from our acceptance and reaction to the frustration of others. When we react instead of respond to the frustration of others, we invite additional negativity in our lives. This interaction may be deemed as frustrating due to the perception we choose. However, if we choose to perceive the interaction in a different light, the interaction and the individual will be perceived differently, thus creating positive alternative possibilities.

When we are willing to examine other alternatives based on the lessons we have learned from past experiences, we invite the potential for positive energy to flow into our lives. Consequently, we will choose to perceive others and situations in a different light, thus allowing our minds to become accessible to other possibilities beyond what we once vehemently decided to retain. This interaction will enable us to subjugate and maintain control of the interaction.

Unchecked and out of control emotions are a major source of negativity. This loss of control is based on a frustrated state of mind and most certainly will invite negative energy into our lives. Maintaining control of our emotions will reduce and eliminate the frustration and consequently the negativity. When we choose to view the experience with a new perspective, believing and knowing that the ultimate outcome will unfold as we desire, we will find that a reason for frustration never existed. Focusing on the negativity in the now, that is the present negative results, will only serve to create additional negativity and consequently frustration. Conversely, focusing on the positive future end results, while using the immediate results as feedback, will generate a state of mind that remains and retains positive momentum.

Which emotions produce your biggest source of negative energy?

How will your life improve by gaining control over your emotions?

Notes:

Date:_____

NO ONE CAN BELITTLE YOU IF YOU HAVE NOT ALREADY BELITTLED YOURSELF

I magine sitting at a family function, enjoying the good food and having a great time. Along comes one of your relatives who subsequently make an "inappropriate" comment that was directed at you. What do you do? The resulting outcome will now depend on what you choose to do next. The course of action you choose will actually depend on the value you have of yourself. This comment will either affect you negatively or you will remain unaffected depending on whether or not you see some truth or validity as it applies to you.

No matter which types of negative comments are thrown at you, they will only stick if the mold has already been created in your mind by you. If you react to a negative comment, you are actually acting out of fear and attempting to defend yourself against the revelation of the presence of this negative comment that has already been created in your mind. Therefore, your reactions are frantic and argumentative. They are simply a protective mechanism to conceal your own despair at the presence of the negative comment that you have intentionally or unintentionally created in your mind. Your intention here is to create a diversion in hopes that others will not recognize its presence.

On the other hand, when you respond to a negative comment, there is a defined thought process involved, based on a higher level of belief. The response will not be frantic and argumentative. Instead of instinctually reacting out of fear, you will choose to respond based on the knowledge and belief in your own abilities. At this point there is neither a need nor a desire to make a point or to prove anything, because your focus is not on what others think of you, but rather what you think of yourself.

If you already have the perception that you are less than others, your reaction will be based on:

a) The emotional pain you are already experiencing from the previous existence of this perception, whether known or unknown

b) The intentional or unintentional highlighting of this previous perception in the present.

This reaction will probably either be explosive or submissive based on your personality type. However, if you considered yourself to be extremely valuable to yourself, you will not react, but will choose to respond to the negative comments with calmness and clarity.

It is an unfortunate human condition that people belittle those who have a high positive perception of themselves. The very high perception of self generates the belittling reaction from others. When you allow others to belittle you, you are activating the pre-formulated belief that you not only deserve to be belittled, but do not deserve to be treated better. This is your current reality; therefore, your subsequent thoughts and actions will bring life to this perception. Others will continue to belittle you, because you have accepted a lesser valuation of self and your actions clearly display this belief.

♥ No one can belittle or degrade you unless you decide to grant them permission to do so!

You are the creator of your life and therefore dictate the view of yourself that others will see. Therefore, it is extremely important to ensure that the vision that you have of yourself expresses a true picture of who you really desire. It may seem difficult at first to change the current vision of yourself, but by embracing the importance of doing so while realizing how it relates to your overall well-being, you will endeavor to rectify this as quickly as possible.

Do you allow others to belittle you?

If so, why do you possess a lesser image of yourself?

Notes:

Date:_____

IF YOUR MIND IS NOT FULL THEN IT MUST BE EMPTY

Mindfulness is the process of continuously monitoring and maintaining thoughts and emotions that are positively constructive and empowering; the prime objective being the management of your direction in relationship to your goal. Please pay attention to the word "continuous". It denotes an ongoing process without room for neglect. Unfortunately, many may believe that the process of continuously monitoring your thoughts is impossible; it simply is too much work. However, the process of mindfulness must never be viewed as a chore. Case in point, if each of us viewed walking as a chore when we were infants, we would surely not be walking today! Initially, walking was difficult and seemed impossible, but through constant practice, we were able to master the process. Likewise, if we believe that our thoughts are instrumental in the creation of our lives, the value we place on the result of our lives will promote the continuous process of mindfulness.

Thoughts that are allowed to flow unchecked produce a life that flows unchecked, whereas, thoughts that flow in harmony with your positive intentions produce a life that flows harmoniously. In order to become cognizant of the types of thoughts we have at any given moment, we MUST first engage in the monitoring process that identifies and brings these thoughts to the forefront of our conscious mind. Then and only then can they be analyzed and compared to the types of thoughts required for the achievement of our goal.

There is no room for disempowering thoughts and diversions. The determination and resolve to actualize our goals must be strong within us and nothing must stand in our way.

On the other hand, mindlessness is the process of continuously maintaining the absence of positively constructive thought while maintaining the presence of destructive thought that direct us away from your goal. Our thoughts are not continuously monitored to ensure that they are directing us in the direction of our goal. Any amount of neglect in mindfulness relinquishes our ability to control the outcome of our lives based on the intention of our desires. Our lives will seemingly flow haphazardly without direction because we are not aware of the types of thoughts that are influencing its direction.

Whenever our minds are filled with thoughts that are leading us towards our goal, it produces more of the same types of thoughts. Conversely, whenever our minds are filled with thoughts that are leading us away from our goal, it produces more of the same types of thoughts. Therefore, it is imperative to continually practice a lifestyle of mindfulness. As soon as we allow a subtle thought of negativity or disbelief to enter our minds, we are manufacturing a harvesting ground in which more of the same will flourish. Remember, thoughts of negativity and disbelief can only be created when the fundamental belief of disbelief is present. Thus, these thoughts are only the symptoms of an even greater disease of disbelief in our system of beliefs.

The practice of mindfulness does not only involve the creation and retention of empowering thoughts through the inclusion of positive beliefs, but is also inclusive of the recognition of ideas, solutions and opportunities. It does not promote the mere operation on a daily basis without an observation of the world around us. Mindfulness further emphasizes the function that opportunities and the answers to our questions abound and are readily available. It encourages a continuous reading of the signs that result from our interaction with the world inside and outside of us as well as our interactions with others. These interactions must subsequently and habitually be analyzed for clues to increase the fulfillment of our lives. A person who is mindful is not concerned about satisfying the cravings for instant gratification and ego nor is he or she willing to succumb to any type of limiting beliefs, because these actions will not offer true fulfillment and receipt of their desires.

The main element that holds the attention of the mindless is negativity. They are void of new ideas and opportunities because of their perpetual engagement in the same old stagnant ideas of the past that do not work, while simultaneously focusing on the frustration created by these ideas that do not work. They do not recognize the opportunities and solutions that are right in front of them because they are too busy complaining about the situation in which they have placed themselves. When asked about the rationale for this ideology, they become experts at generating excuses as they begin to hastily assert a myriad of amazing and gravity defying tales of woe and atrocities. The responsibility for their own lives never rests on them, because it is immediately deflected onto another person, place or thing. Little do they know or realize that the very answer or opportunity they seek may be literally in front of them, but is illusive because of their self-created obstruction.

Being in a mindless state is tantamount to running on autopilot without an initial flight check. The course is laid in, but unbeknownst, there is little room for a margin of error because the flight was doomed from the start. Whenever an adjustment needs to be made, disaster is sure to be imminent, because the original course plan did not take into consideration the ever changing landscape that led to the intended destination. On the other hand, mindfulness is an ever changing process of progression. It is a lifestyle of constantly monitoring your flight plan and conditions, appropriately adjusting when necessary.

There are no ifs, ands or buts about mindfulness. You are either mindful or you are not. You either value the attainment of your desires or you do not. Whenever your mind is not filled with thoughts based on the attainment of your desires, it is void of all ability to achieve these desires, much less true fulfillment. A mind devoid of all focus cannot create a life that is filled with focus. A life not filled with focus is a life that cannot produce even a single desire of the mind.

Do you value the lifestyle of mindfulness?

How can mindfulness improve your life?

Notes:

Date:_____

GARBAGE INTO THE MIND; GARBAGE OUT OF THE MIND

W e are all familiar with the computer cliché "garbage in, garbage out". Well, the mind is no different. It is like a computer system; it can only process what it is given. If it is fed garbage, do not expect to receive anything but garbage. There is a common misconception that our lives result mostly from actions that are out of our control, when in fact our lives are a direct and indirect result of the details that we add to it. These details include all of the beliefs and thoughts that we have about our lives. When inserted into the complex matrix of our minds, these beliefs and thoughts will produce a result depending on the types of beliefs and thoughts that it was originally fed.

There are so many avenues that garbage can enter the mind. Many of them are extremely subtle in nature because they have become intertwined with our accepted form of everyday life. The notion that we should continue to accept the inclusion of limiting beliefs in our lives is but one example. The continued acceptance of the limiting beliefs of the past and present are like a cornucopia of debris we adhere to so dearly, while ironically regarding them as treasure.

If our actions are not producing the correct results, we are harboring garbage under the guise of treasure. When we engage in habitually destructive patterns of behavior, we are hoarding trash and debris in the crevices of our minds.

Garbage into the mind is any belief, thought or predetermination that is based on our fears and frustrations. For example,

▶ The belief that bad things will always happen or that a life of abundance will never be achieved is actually garbage information that is fed into the mind.

▶ Disempowering thoughts related to non-deserving of a life of abundance or limitations of self-worth are garbage thoughts that are fed into the mind.

▶ The predeterminations that life will be exactly as it was in the past without any possibility of improvement are garbage thoughts.

In simple terms, these are all disempowering thoughts that only serve to divert us away from our goal. How can we possibly expect to arrive at our destination when we are adding water to our gas in hopes of getting more miles per gallon? You just will not make it. Likewise, when any amount of negativity is an additive to our minds, the output of our lives will be exactly what we are feeding our mind; we will not achieve our desired goal.

Even though we may originally perceive something as "impossible", our perception does not have to be static. If we are willing to explore options that are outside of our predetermined comfort zone, absolutely decide on our success and believe in the possibility of this success, our perception WILL change. With this change in perception, the outcome of our lives will also change. If we allow our perception to remain static, we will automatically foster negativity. This is the garbage that we allow to enter our minds. Our situation certainly will not improve when we are fearful, frustrated, complacent and complain. The only way to rectify the situation is to be continually mindful of what we are feeding our minds on a daily basis. This will ensure that the outcome of our lives will be in accordance to our desires.

What types of garbage thoughts are you feeding your mind?

How can you conduct housekeeping to purge your mind of these thoughts by changing your beliefs?

Notes:

Date:_____

IF YOU DESIRE X, THEN X MUST DOMINATE YOUR EVERY THOUGHT AND NOTHING ELSE

There are many types of thoughts that are created or allowed to enter our minds on a daily basis. However, whether these thoughts are positive or negative is determined and fueled by our current beliefs. Our core beliefs not only function as a creator of our current thoughts but also as a barometer of what is accepted or rejected in order to construct our perception of reality. Thus, if we have a particular desire, but do not believe that it is possible or that we deserve it, the types of thoughts that will dominate our minds will be those that propel us further away from actualizing our desires. This will create our perception of our reality; a life of constant struggles. On the other hand, if we (a) truly believe that our desires are possible and (b) believe that we deserve them, our thoughts will be focused solely on the achievement of our desires.

The process of receiving involves a strong belief and acceptance of our desires as though we have already received them. This process may seem difficult and counterintuitive, but the results are overwhelmingly powerful. When we believe as though we have already received our desires, all traces of doubt and fear are eliminated from the constructs of our core beliefs. This in turn causes the creation of empowering thoughts which envelopes and expands our perception for the recognition of opportunities and solutions. Our subsequent actions are automatically driven by these empowering thoughts to produce that which we already believe.

The reason it appears extremely difficult to believe as though we have already received is because our current beliefs are limited by our predeterminations. These predeterminations are based on our own internal limiting beliefs and the limiting beliefs of others. For example, "only do what you are supposed to do"; "it is difficult to do that"; "only rich people can afford that" and "trying to make ends meet" are some of the many limiting beliefs that bombard us from the time we were born. No wonder our lives are filled with limitation; we are conditioned to be limited from birth. Even when we have desires that exceed the status quo, our limiting predeterminations begin to wage a skirmish against our thoughts of enlightenment in order to preserve their own survival. The "little" voices we hear in our minds that incite disbelief and thoughts of non-deserving and not being good enough are prime examples of this skirmish.

As this war ensues, the cultivation of our thoughts relative to our desires is slowly eroded. One moment we may have empowering thoughts and then the next moment we may have thoughts of fear and. If we allow these distractive thoughts to perpetuate, we will never reach our true potential and as such never actualize our desires. The disempowering thoughts of fear and disbelief will ultimately overrule our empowering thoughts of success.

Our full attention must be fastened on only what we desire! By allowing detrimental thoughts to flow through our minds, we are literally disempowering the thoughts that are providing passage to our goals. Anything that is diluted is not as strong as its undiluted counterpart. Likewise, the empowering thoughts based on mindfulness, believing and knowing will be weakened anytime we engage in beliefs based on non-deserving, fear and frustration. In order to achieve our desires, we must build a momentum that is based solely on the thoughts that are actively bringing us closer to our goals and immediately eliminate those thoughts that are diluting our empowering thoughts. No room must be allocated for doubt and fear. If success is desired, only thoughts related to success must dominate the mind, leaving no room for doubt and disbelief.

Do the desires of your life dominate your thought?

What limiting predeterminations diminish these thoughts?

Notes:

Date:_____

GOODNESS IS NOT GAINED BY FOCUSING ON EVIL; WELLNESS IS NOT GAINED BY FOCUSING ON SICKNESS

Our society has trained and conditioned us to focus mainly on the negative most of the time. Typically, we focus and gravitate more towards negatively charged thinking as opposed to gravitating towards positively charged thinking. A classic example of this can be seen in the typical focus on the "problem" and not the solution. Characteristically, our focus tends to be on the perceived lack in our lives as opposed to the elimination of this perceived lack and the production of emotions based on our enjoyment of our available life of abundance. For example, if we stated to friends, family and peers that we desired to start a new business, most would probably furnish admonitions instead of congratulatory accolades. If we desired to try something new, most people would prescribe warnings as opposed to endorsements. Granted our society is based on protectionism, but it is also based on thinking entirely within the box.

Many of us desire a life of abundance; however our beliefs, thoughts and actions speak volumes that are contrary to this life of abundance. We desire to live a good life but we consistently engage in negative thinking. We desire to be healthy, but we consistently focus on not being sick as opposed to focusing on being healthy. There are strong subtleties in what we desire in life and what we actually focus on. For example, if we desire a large beautiful home, but instead our attention is focused on our perceived inability to obtain this home, our beliefs and thoughts are actually focused on our perceived lack of available funds to purchase this home. We will always receive what we are focusing on; the lack of available funds to purchase our desired home. This is the mental trap that shackles our lives to continuous limitations and non-fulfillment.

Many of our physical ailments come as a result of our beliefs and the thoughts that pervade our mind. We focus on not getting sick instead of focusing on being healthy. As subtle as this may sound, if our focus is on not being sick, then sickness and the fear associated with being sick is a core highlight of our focus. On the other hand, if we are focusing on always being healthy, then being healthy and the good emotions associated with it will be our core focus. These simple subtleties have a huge impact on our lives because they are actually directives that either foster growth or initiate destruction in our lives.

The goodness of life and all that it has to offer cannot be obtained when we are thinking in ways that are contrary and opposing to a life of goodness. Since a life of goodness requires a specific way of thinking, any beliefs that produce contrary and opposing thoughts will produce a life that is contrary to a life of goodness. Contradictory thoughts always abound in the absence of true belief. Thoughts of fear always proliferate in the absence of belief. When true belief is present, we will not make the subtle mistake of desiring goodness while simultaneously harboring thoughts of disbelief; desiring wellness but focusing on the fear of being sick. Through mindfulness we can continually ensure that our thoughts, no matter how subtle they may appear, are always keeping us on track towards our goal.

Are you seeking goodness but focusing on a perceived lack?

How are your contradictory thoughts affected by your level of belief or disbelief?

Notes:

Date:_____

NEGATIVITY IS LIKE A PARASITIC GERM. IT EATS AWAY AT YOUR CORE UNTIL THERE IS NOTHING LEFT

Are you familiar with someone who is extremely negative? You can be extremely vibrant before you speak to such a person however, when you are in their presence, your spirit and energy gets zapped immediately. It is as though they drained the very life force from you. Their negativity has now become your negativity. Their bad mood has now become your bad mood. It is as though their very negative essence is highly contagious and no matter how you try to avoid its effect, your state of mind becomes affected as a result of the exposure. Eventually you may regain your positive momentum but continued exposure for undue lengths of time will eventually render you vulnerable to the same types of thoughts.

If this negativity is allowed to fester through continued exposure to it, it will grow exponentially like a parasitic virus and consume you. Your desire to improve your life will be drained until you have only enough energy to simply exist. Your goals, dreams and aspirations will evaporate. Due to the highly contagious nature of negativity, once initialized, it will spread like wildfire. It can start out simply like a little speck, highly unnoticeable and often times ignored because of its apparent lack in size and momentum. But even the smallest speck of negativity in your mind carries with it the potential to not only attract other negative thoughts, but also produce them as well. You attract other negative thoughts through association. As a result your negative thoughts produce the negative choices and actions that you make in your life, which in turn creates the type of life you are currently experiencing. Others who are experiencing a similar type of lifestyle will be attracted to you by the apparent common interests.

A profound method that negativity uses to enslave is through self-creation and self-proliferation. The types of thoughts you foster will serve to produce similar complementary thoughts which aid its proliferation. Therefore, if you foster positive thoughts, additional positive thoughts will be created. On the other hand, if you foster negative thoughts, you will automatically produce more of the same. Negative thoughts are created by the mere existence of other negative thoughts. When you foster negativity, you are actively participating in the creation of negativity in your life. Also, the mere existence of negative thoughts passively creates additional negativity in your life.

However, when both negative and positive thoughts are present, the thoughts that are assigned the most value (i.e. a belief in the possibility of its realization) will be the thoughts that will be prevalent in your mind. All thought, whether they are negative or positive, is assigned a value of belief. The greater the belief that your life will unfold according to a specific thought, the greater the value you will place on the thought. For example, if both positive and negative thoughts are present and a higher value is placed on the negative thoughts, you will end up in a negative state of mind because the amount of negative thoughts produced outweighs the amount of positive thoughts. This may result in a pendulum between a highly positive state of mind at times to a highly negative state of mind at other times. Thus, it is extremely important to not only maintain your mental positivity through mindfully

fostering only positive thoughts, but also to continually surround yourself with those who are positive as well. You are
not only what you believe yourself to be, but your life will
also be based on the type of people with whom you are associated and the situations you create or in which you become
involved. Remember, if you desire to avoid having a parasitic
germ – avoid negativity!

Do you engage in negative thinking on a daily basis?

If so, how are these types of thoughts helping you to improve your life?

Notes:

Date:_____

NEGATIVITY NEEDS YOU TO SURVIVE. YOU DO NOT NEED IT TO SURVIVE

Y ou are in control of whatever form and level of negativity you have in your mind or choose to be exposed to! Consequently, you can decide if it continues to play a function in your life. The choice is always up to you. Even when your life seems to be in total disarray and you perceive that your options are extremely limited, there are still so many other choices that you can make that will bring positivity into your life and eliminate the current barrage of negativity. It is simply a matter of intentionally believing in the face of adversity, while simultaneously knowing that the end result will be in accordance to your focused vision of success.

Your disempowering thoughts are formulated as a result of your accepted beliefs from your past experiences. The basis for your perception is what you believe as defined by your past experiences and what you choose to accept as true from these past experiences. Any time your core beliefs are filled with doubt and fear, you are focusing on doubt and fear, thus placing more value on the production of the same. For this reason, these disempowering thoughts are continually being produced in your mind. Your limiting beliefs are literally perpetuating these thoughts.

The beliefs of doubt, non-deserving, frustration and fear

to name a few, are all fundamentally limiting beliefs that automatically produce disempowering thoughts. No matter how much you try to struggle against these disempowering thoughts, your battle will be futile because you are attacking the symptom and not the root problem. You are only masking the regeneration of negativity through your attempts at thinking positively. The root problem itself stems from what you believe is true and possible, all of which originate from your earliest childhood experiences. To change these thoughts, you must first change what you have grown accustomed to believing and accepting as true. Then and only then can you begin to replace the disempowering thoughts that have taken root in your mind.

Any time you have disempowering thoughts in your mind, they will attempt to replace any previous or current empowering thoughts. In order for negativity to continue to flourish in your mind, you must continually feed it with more like thoughts. Negativity spreads with the more attention and focus you give to it. It is created by you and within you. Whenever you focus your attention on the "problem" and the frustrations associated with the "problem", you are feeding and nurturing your negativity. The "problem" gets bigger and bigger with every passing moment that you continue to nurture it with your negative attention and focus.

Negativity needs its creator to feed it in order for it to survive. If you alter your current beliefs, your disempowering thoughts will continually decrease and they will eventually starve and die. You do not need negative thoughts to survive; otherwise all of the people with positive thoughts would have long since died. Your negativity needs you to feed it for it to live, not the other way around. Similar to most things in our lives, we need practice in order to build proficiency. At first it may seem to be difficult until you become acclimated to the process. However, with each passing day it becomes easier and easier. Likewise, with negativity, you must practice a reduction in your negative thinking through an alteration of your current beliefs until your thoughts are positively aligned.

Will you continue to live without having any negative thoughts?

What do you think would happen if you engaged in believing positively?

Notes:

Date:_____

THOUGHTS OF NEGATIVITY ARE LIKE A FREEFALLING OBJECT... THEY INCREASE IN SPEED AS TIME PASSES

I f you dropped a bowling ball from a ten story build-ing, it will begin from its place of rest in your hand, to a maximum speed governed by gravity. As the bowling ball travels towards the ground, it will increase in speed; you no longer have control over where it will fall. The sheer momentum that the bowling ball experiences as it falls towards the ground will increase the longer it is allowed to fall. Additionally, the amount of collateral damage that is sus-tained as a result of the falling bowling ball will also increase the longer the bowling ball is allowed to fall.

Your negative thoughts are no different; they are like the bowling ball at rest when they surface, but they quickly gain speed and momentum once they are let go. Once you allow your negative thoughts to fall freely, you gradually lose your ability to control them and they will eventually start to control you. The amount of momentum that your negative thoughts produce will also increase, the longer YOU expose yourself or are allowed to be exposed to these types of thoughts. This momentum is the driving force that jumpstarts the ability to perpetuate itself causing your negative thoughts to feed itself as they reproduce more negative thoughts. Additionally, the amount of collateral damage that is sustained as a result of your negative thoughts will also increase, the longer they are allowed to develop and fester in your mind.

The more negative thoughts you have, the more negative thoughts you will have.

Your negative thoughts are derived and driven by your limiting and fear based beliefs. These beliefs will cause you to react instinctually out of fear instead of responding based on a belief in your vision of your success; the result will inevitably produce undesirable experiences in your life. *Negativity feeds off of negativity. It must produce more negativity in order for it to survive.* Have you ever noticed how your mind becomes even more chaotic as soon as you allow a single thought based on fear to run rapidly through your mind? This is because of the momentum that is produced by the single negative thought. If you do not take steps to eliminate the negative thoughts as soon as they surface, they will eventually destroy your life.

When negative thoughts, no matter how small, surface in your mind, you must immediately contemplate the absolute origin of these thoughts. Which beliefs and fears are actually driving these thoughts? They must be addressed, otherwise you will only address the symptom and not the root cause; the negative thoughts will resurface once again. Oftentimes we may utilize instant gratification as a form of release; however, we are simply addressing the symptom and not the actual cause. Whenever you address the symptom and not the root cause, you are leaving yourself vulnerable and susceptible to future attacks. Your negative thoughts are derived and driven by your fears and your fears are derived and driven by what you believe is possible in your life. In order to eliminate this negativity, you must eliminate the fear and in order to eliminate the fear you must eliminate the destructive beliefs that are producing and perpetuating your fears.

How many negative thoughts do you have on a daily basis?

What would happen if you were able to drastically decrease these thoughts?

Notes:

Date:_____

A LIFE OF ABUNDANCE IS NOT GAINED BY THINKING AND FOCUSING ON POVERTY

Poverty consciousness runs rampant in our society. When I refer to poverty consciousness, I am in part denoting the beliefs that many of us have about money and our ability to obtain it. Money in its simplest form is just paper, but in its intended form is a system of exchange. This system allows us to exchange the medium of money for the goods and services which we desire. But since money is merely a medium by which trade is initiated, why do we possess such a stigmatism concerning is use and attainment? Why do some people have more of it while others have far less? Why does it flow "effortlessly" to some and sparingly to others? The common denominator resides in one's belief system as it relates to money.

When you possess a fundamental belief in your vision of success and you are committed to this vision, you "know" that you will attain your goal because of your "intimate relationship" with your vision of success. Money is fully embraced and not resisted because your vision of success includes the immediate replenishment of this medium. There is no reason to be concerned about the amount that is available to you because there is an abundance supply available to you. However, when you either lack a specific vision of success; disbelieve in any aspect of this vision of success; create resistance in your life through the use of your limiting beliefs and thoughts of the past and/or possess a chaotic and frustrated state of mind, you literally fear the use of money because of a concern about its potential replenishment. For example, if you had $100,000 in your bank account and were contemplating the purchase of an $80,000 Mercedes, the level of fear in the purchase will be directly dependent on your level of belief in the immediate replenishment of the $80,000.

If you believed that you would immediately receive a replenishment, the purchase probably would not faze you. On the other hand if you believed that a replenishment was relatively unlikely or nowhere in sight, you would probably elect to conserve as much money as possible. However, if you truly believed in your success, why wouldn't you be able to induce a replenishment with the remaining $20,000? You could probably use the $20,000 to start a business. Here again your limiting beliefs may interject thoughts of fear and disbelief in your ability and possibility of starting a successful business using the $20,000. Your concern undoubtedly would be the complete depletion of all of your available funds. But the possibility of success should not incite questions of disbelief. Others were able to build successful businesses out of their garages with far less than $20,000; therefore the possibility of success should not be in question. The underlying notion is your level of belief in the attainment of more, which essentially is a focus on lack.

In everyday life, it seems as though our outlay of money is always far greater than our intake of money. The situation seems to leave us in a constant state of flux because most individuals are either concerned about just being able to pay their bills or having sufficient money left over after the bills are paid to take a vacation hopefully once a year. The notion of this mechanism leads to the perception that there is never enough money to go around when in actuality there is more than enough money to go around because money in itself is just a means of bartering goods and services. When we live our lives with the mechanistic view that we will never have enough money to satisfy our desires, this perception becomes our reality. Therefore, we will never have enough to satisfy our desires.

On the other hand, if we believe and perceive that we will have more than enough, our thoughts and actions will be different from those based on a focus on the lack of money. Those who do not believe that they will have enough are satisfied with remaining in their current position in a complacent state. On the other hand those who believe and perceive that they will have more than enough will not act or behave in a complacent state but will however seek out opportunities or create their own opportunities to make their belief a reality.

Thinking in poverty is synonymous to foregoing the expenditure on a $50 cooking pot while spending $25 every three months for a cheap replacement. You postulate that you are saving money by not spending the $50 because you believe that you will never receive sufficient funds to quickly replace the $50 if spent, when in actuality you are spending much more by having to constantly replace the inferior cooking pot. The money to replace the inferior pot three times amounts to $75, which is more than the $50 you originally believed you could not easily replace. Your belief found a way to produce the $75, therefore your belief will find a way to quickly replenish far less than the $75.

This type of poverty consciousness stems from our lack of belief that we have the ability to open multiple doors of opportunity for ourselves. When one door closes another will open automatically or by our doing as long as we do not resist it with our fears and disbelief.

What are your inhibitions about money?

Do you feel as though it is difficult to obtain? Why?

Notes:

Date:_____

THINKING IN POVERTY CAUSES YOU TO LIVE IN POVERTY

Whatever a man or woman believes about themselves is exactly what they will receive. We cannot believe that we will always be poor and then expect to be rich, nor can we believe that thoughts of non-deserving and not being good enough will bring us closer to a life of abundance. These are contradictory thoughts that offer resistance to our ability to receive our desires. No wonder many of us are frustrated with our current situation. We have not taken the time to analyze our past and current beliefs, thoughts and behavioral habits and how they affect our current lives.

Poverty can be broken down into two major components, (a) mental and (b) physical poverty.

a) Mental poverty is an enslavement of the mind, which creates a state of mind that produces and regenerates self-limiting and disempowering thoughts. These thoughts originate from within but are also influenced by the limiting thoughts accepted from others. The opportunities and solutions that are readily available cannot even be comprehended because they are out of scope and appear to be out of range. The mind is enslaved and will not venture beyond what is believed to be possible.

b) Physical poverty is a direct result of mental poverty. Physical poverty is not only akin to the creation of negative experiences related to the body but also embodies the creation of negative experiences in the "world" around us. It is inclusive of such elements as time, money and relationships. These elements are affected by the level of mental poverty one possesses. For example, physical poverty as it relates to our current financial situation is the application of mental poverty that adversely affects our living condition, the food we eat, the type of car we drive and so on. There is unnecessary sacrifice and hardship because of a focus on lack and perceived limitations. Physical poverty as it relates to relationships is also the creation of negativity that adversely affects our relationships through the belief and perception that the present and future will be exactly like the past. We fill our present relationships with the self-defeating thoughts that were migrated from the past without analyzing ourselves to determine how OUR thoughts and actions are contributing to the experiences in the present.

Note that when there is mental poverty, physical poverty is automatically a by-product. Likewise, when there is a continuous immersion in physical poverty, mental poverty is automatically reinforced. Both types of poverty are interrelated and intertwined. One will affect the other.

If we believe that our lives will always be filled with difficulty and poverty, the thoughts produced will be related to the validation of this belief and our emotions and actions will resonate harmoniously with these thoughts.

We will not focus on the solutions and opportunities available to help us achieve our life of abundance, but we will continue to complain about the "problems" on which we are solely focused. The resulting complacency will prohibit us from even attempting to find solutions and opportunities, since we will consider them to be non-existent. This forms the basis of our "reality".

History is filled with many individuals who have braved all odds to make a mark in this world. While others lacked absolute belief in their ideas and abilities, they instead resolved to find solutions and opportunities instead of complaining in misery. If they did not believe that their desires were possible; they never would have continued to think thoughts relative to their success. Likewise, our life of abundance can only be attained by first believing in the attainment of our success. The correct use of the power of belief in the face of adversity will entirely change our lives. However, it will take a daily regimen of mindfulness to undo the old beliefs and thoughts of the past; but when we are focused only on the benefits that our success WILL bring, we will not become frustrated.

Remember, in order to live a life of abundance both physically and mentally, we must first believe that it is possible. This belief will continue to foster thoughts that empower our lives. If we desire to achieve a particular goal, we must constantly believe and subsequently think thoughts related to the achievement of this goal. We must refrain from thoughts related to the non-achievement of this goal, because in doing so, we directly sabotage our every move. We must look internally and examine our own beliefs and thoughts to define how they have influenced our actions in the past and are currently influencing our actions in the present. By examining our past experiences relevant to our past beliefs, thoughts and actions, we will uncover those instances that set the precedent and continue to influence our lives.

Are you currently thinking in poverty?

If so what are some of these destructive thoughts?

Notes:

Date:_____

MOST PEOPLE WILL REMAIN "POOR" NOT BECAUSE OF THEIR INABILITY TO BECOME RICH, BUT BECAUSE OF THEIR LACK OF PROSPERITY CONSCIOUSNESS

Most people are not physically limited from attaining wealth, but ironically they limit their ability to become wealthy by placing limits on their beliefs and thoughts, which in turn disables them both physically and mentally. Some individuals may possess talents and abilities that can easily be cultivated to produce large amounts of wealth while others may have access to resources that can explode their financial growth; however their current financial situation still lingers in ruin. The question here is not whether they are incapable of becoming wealthy but rather how are their beliefs and thoughts offering resistance to their ability to attain wealth.

As a fundamental rule, an individual who desires to become wealthy cannot have the beliefs and thoughts and actions of a person who has accepted poverty as their lot in life. By doing so, they remain relegated to a life of lack because their focus is fixated on a life of lack. Since specific beliefs, specific thoughts and specific actions will bring about specific results, a life of wealth can only be attained by adopting the specific beliefs, thoughts and actions associated with wealth. In Principle, if you continually think in poverty, you are thinking in contrast to prosperity consciousness.

Poverty consciousness is a way of life that fosters the thinking that your present will contain the same level of lack as your past and your future will contain the same level of lack as your present. Poverty consciousness also includes at its very core a belief that money available today will not be readily available tomorrow. This assumption violates the universal laws of prosperity. Our purpose in life is to live in prosperity. Our world has been designed with this abundant supply philosophy in mind. The trees; the production of oxygen; the sun; all are prime examples of perpetual production for our enjoyment and sustenance. When we think and focus on our perceived lack, that is all we will perceive and that is all we will achieve.

Prosperity consciousness however is not to be confused with a lifestyle that is lavishly wasteful. Prosperity consciousness signifies the abolition of a perception of a continuous present and future lack. It also incorporates a fundamental belief that there is always an abundant supply available. It is a belief that if the source of one supply decreases, another will surely increase; when one door closes two more will be opened. The individual who practices prosperity consciousness will not view their current financial situation with fear and frustration because they believe and know that another source of bounty is available to them. They value the elimination of fear and frustration; for it is through these destructive forces that other sources of abundance are kept hidden and concealed from view.

A classic example that fueled a need for a change in my way of thinking can be traced back to the many mistakes I made in my career. For example, prior to my enlightenment, the biggest mistake that I made in my real estate career was not being mindful of my beliefs, thoughts and actions during the purchasing process. I believed that I had to purchase as many properties as quickly as possible, but I neglected to be mindful of my ability to maintain and repair all of these properties in a timely manner. I was operating based on poverty consciousness because my focus was on a perceived lack of available deals in the future as well as a perceived lack of my ability to successfully arrive at my goal. Shortly afterwards the market crashed and I was stuck with lots of overpriced properties in a market filled with an abundant supply of extremely cheap properties.

The perception that you will not be able to achieve abundance in your life will affect everything that you say and do. You will neglect to foster thoughts and actions relative to abundance because of the perception that you will never attain abundance. Naturally you will never attain a life of abundance because your thoughts and actions are contrary to a life of abundance. When we think in poverty consciousness, thoughts of a lack of replenishment and thoughts questioning the existence of an abundant supply will cause us to formulate choices that will deter us away from our goal.

Do you believe you have the ability to achieve wealth?

_____

_____

How do your thoughts of lack offer resistance to the attainment of this wealth?

_____

_____

Notes:

_____

_____

_____

_____

_____

_____

Date:_____

STRUGGLING WITH THE THOUGHT OF GETTING THE HONDA WILL NOT GET YOU THE MERCEDES

I f you cannot imagine it or if you have a problem think-ing that you deserve it, then how can you achieve it? If thoughts of frustration initiated by your perceived lack thereof are causing you to have a limited vision, your life of abundance will not come to you. As you perpetuate the lim-iting beliefs set in your own mind by you, your limitations will force you to think in limitations and behave as though you are absolutely limited.

A life of abundance calls for a prescribed method of be-lieving, thinking and choosing the appropriate actions. This prescribed method does not include any type of limiting be-liefs, limiting thoughts and limiting behaviors. When you set limitations on yourself, you are not acting in accordance with your desired life of abundance. The human body cannot flour-ish when its water and food supply is restricted; neither can your desires flourish when it is restricted by your beliefs.

The amount of money currently in your bank account may not be sufficient to purchase the Mercedes but you do not have to settle for the Honda if you truly believe that you deserve the Mercedes and that attaining it is possible. Just because the money is not currently in plain sight does not mean that it is unavailable. By focusing on what you desire and not on your perceived limitations, you allow your mind to remain open to the recognition of opportunities that abound around you and the creation of new and exciting opportunities and possibilities.

Moving beyond your self-inflicted limitations first involves a desire and a willingness to recognize and embrace the fact that you are the creator of your life and you have the ability to remove the limitations from your life since they were constructed by you initially. Once you embrace this realization, you must begin to focus your attention on your desires while paying special attention to your emotions. Your emotions, for example, your level of frustration, will monitor your overall progress and will indicate when an adjustment in your beliefs, thoughts and action is needed. Know and believe that your overall desires will be achieved regardless of the interim situations. If you cannot see beyond your current perceived limitations, you will remain limited in every aspect of your life.

Oftentimes we settle in life not because of our inability to achieve what we desire, but because of a decision to settle. This decision comes as a result of what we believe is possible. This belief in our ability to achieve a life of abundance is tested on a daily basis and must be continually monitored and adjusted when necessary. Any contradictory, non-deserving and limiting beliefs will disrupt your ability to consistently think thoughts relative to the attainment of your life of abundance. These contradictory thoughts will trick us into thinking that we can only afford or deserve the 10-year-old Honda and not the brand new Mercedes-Benz. It is entirely about what we believe is possible in our lives that will make our desires possible and true. When we are continually mindful of these contradictory thoughts, we are actively engaging in the process of circumventing the possibility of disbelief from entering our minds.

What are your current beliefs about what you deserve in life?

How can you change these beliefs so that you can realize your desires?

Notes:

Date:_____

SUCCESS IS A STATE OF MIND... FAILURE IS A DIFFERENT STATE OF MIND

The state of mind that you have at any given point in time is based on what you believe. Your state of mind encompasses such things as not only what you believe, but also your fears, your inhibitions, your joys and your sorrows based on these beliefs. These elements all come together to formulate your current state of mind. Even though these elements may appear to be absolute, they are subject to change at any given point based on a direct decision to make a change. Therefore, your current state of mind is always subject to change because the elements that make up your current state of mind are subject to change.

When you create a vision of your life of success in your mind and completely believe in this vision of success, you are adjusting the parameters of your current state of mind to perceive your life of success through the elimination of your fear based thoughts, emotions associated with non-deserving, low self-worth and other disempowering thoughts that contradict your empowering thoughts. A success driven state of mind is not a state of mind built on fear and the emotions associated with non-deserving. A success driven state of mind is built upon a defining belief in your ability to succeed. Your level of belief will directly affect all of the elements that constitute your current state of mind. Therefore, in the presence of disbelief, your fears are increased; your inhibitions are highlighted; your joys are diminished and your sorrows are accentuated. By altering your beliefs to include a commitment to the absolute attainment of your success, you are directly adjusting the way that you think and you are directly adjusting your current state of mind to be in tune with what is required for a life of success. If you can believe in things unseen, then how much more so should you believe in the "unseen" power of your mind to believe in what you desire?

Failure as a created option on the other hand, is a state of mind that is far different from a state of mind based on success. The state of mind based on success and the state of mind based on failure as a created option cannot coexist within the same space because what is required for one is a detriment to the other. A state of mind based on failure as a created option has fear at the heart of its core belief structure. This belief of fear creates paralysis both in your mental and physical state. The end result will inevitably create the very failure which you fear.

If you focus on the attributes of success and the attributes of failure simultaneously, the dichotomy will create frustration and chaos in your mind. There will be a constant struggle between the two groups as each will attempt to survive at the expense of the other. Under these circumstances, your direction in life will depend on your ability to focus on your state of mind of success while eliminating the traits associated with a state of mind based on the creation of failure. Both groups will not coexist simultaneously in harmony. How can you ultimately achieve success when thoughts of failure flow freely through your mind? When you decide to use any unsuccessful attempts at achieving your goal as feedback to aid you in adjusting your current beliefs, you are not viewing these unsuccessful attempts as failures, but merely as measurable feedback. Failure in itself is simply an absolute decision based on the restricting beliefs of your current state of mind. Without the ability to see beyond the perceived current limiting beliefs, failure as a created option seems like the only "logical" choice.

Is your current state of mind built on success?

How can you alter your beliefs to increase your level of success?

Notes:

Date:_____

SUCCESS COMES WHEN YOU ALLOW THOUGHTS OF SUCCESS TO REPLACE THOUGHTS OF FAILURE

In principle, adhering to negativity related to the present is counterproductive. Likewise, holding onto the old negativity of the past will not add any value to your life. Since negativity related to the present is not worth holding onto, adhering to negativity that is years old is even more detrimental. In fact, both the negativity of the past and present will only serve to diminish your true potential and fulfillment in the present and in the future. Think about the detrimental effect imposed on your life when you do not release all of the disempowering beliefs and perceptions of the past. You are simply producing a fertile ground in which more negativity will grow and flourish, overwhelming you in the present and diminishing your future.

When you continue to focus on the old negative experiences of the past, negative emotions associated with them will emerge to the forefront; leaving no room for you to grow. Your mind will be too busy focusing and consequently creating what you believe is <u>your</u> reality; that is, continued negative experiences.

Your past beliefs, thoughts and actions are exactly that… in the past. However, your past missteps, when used as lessons to help you improve your life, are extremely valuable. These missteps, when used as measurable feedback to aid you in the adjustment of your current beliefs, have done what they were intended to do; provide you with valuable life changing lessons. Now, it is time to move on to new and exciting possibilities with the new lessons you have learned at the helm of your life.

Success can only flourish when you have more thoughts of success than failure and allow these thoughts to eventually replace any remaining thoughts of failure.

Success cannot grow in an arena that is crowded by beliefs and thoughts related to the creation of failure. Most notably, thoughts of failure relate to the limiting beliefs associated with past experiences and are typically used to create more of the same instead of being used as insight. However, when **you decide** to build upon the insight gained from the lessons of the past while simultaneously refusing to adhere to the negative emotions associated with this past, (for example, "being hard on yourself"), you are removing the barriers to your success. Your ability to build upon the lessons of the past is directly related to your desire and choice to eliminate the negative emotions associated with the past.

Whenever you change your beliefs to accommodate an expanded view of what is possible in your life, you will automatically relinquish the negative limiting thoughts which are providing resistance to your ability to achieve your goals. You are engaging in a housekeeping process, where you begin to remove the negative clutter and make room for success in your life.

Your current thoughts are built upon previous similar thoughts and one thought, no matter how small, leads to the production of a similar type of thought. In Principle, any amount of negativity or thoughts of failure you allow into your mind brings with it the potential to grow into an unmanageable aspect in your life. When you are mindful of your thoughts and emotions, you become aware that you are engaging in negative thinking and will immediately seek to disrupt this behavior with the intention of eliminating the negative thinking and the negative behavior. Your current beliefs must be reexamined and adjusted to ensure that these disempowering thoughts are removed by the roots and not simply trimmed.

Thoughts of success often appear to be difficult to maintain. The difficulty arises not from the inability to produce and maintain such thoughts, but rather from the conflict between such thoughts and your already deeply rooted negative thoughts. No matter what aspect of your life you are trying to master, you can only master it if you nourish and retain beliefs and thoughts that are constructive and eliminate the beliefs and thoughts that are destructive. Destructive beliefs and thoughts can come in very subtle ways, most of which may be buried deeply within your subconscious. By analyzing your conscious thoughts and actions for clues on why you think and act in a specific way, you can begin to unravel the layers of your subconscious limiting beliefs and thoughts that are constructing your current conscious limiting beliefs and limited thoughts.

Do you have more thoughts of failure than success?

How can you change this belief ratio?

Notes:

Date:_____

WEALTH COMES WHEN THERE ARE MORE THOUGHTS OF WEALTH THAN THOUGHTS OF POVERTY

Wealth comes when there are more thoughts of wealth than there are contradictory poverty conscious thoughts. Every day, each of us may have thoughts that contradict each other both blatantly and subtly. For example, you may have the thought of owning a brand new Mercedes-Benz or a big beautiful home and then immediately have thoughts of lack or non-deserving. Some of the typical thoughts associated with this are, "I will never be able to afford such things", "I do not feel as though I deserve such things" or "Only rich people deserve to own such things". We typically attempt to pacify ourselves by suggesting that we "lower our expectations back down to reality", not realizing that "reality" is what we believe and perceive "reality" to be. There isn't a masked gunman frantically waving a loaded handgun at you, demanding that you limit your beliefs and perceptions. In all reality, you have created your personal masked gunman inside your mind and he is frantically waving a handgun of deceit and compelling you to limit your beliefs and perceptions.

Anytime you possess empowering thoughts that are immediately or eventually followed by opposing thoughts, you are experiencing contradictory thoughts. Depending on the frequency and strength of these contradictory thoughts, they can actually prove to be the deciding factor in your decision making process. Contradictory thoughts always highlight the presence of contradictory beliefs. Contradictory beliefs always highlight the presence of disbelief, hence lack of confidence.

If you have strong empowering thoughts and even stronger contradictory thoughts, the contradictory thoughts will automatically become the dominant deciding factor and directive for your subsequent actions. Likewise, if you possess strong empowering thoughts and equally strong contradictory thoughts, a struggle for supremacy will ensue; the by-product of which is typically frustration. This frustration, depending on how it is used, can undoubtedly add to the current level of contradictory thoughts thus destroying any chance of your empowering thoughts functioning as the ultimate deciding factor for your decisions. But even if your frustration is utilized correctly as feedback for your life, there is still the presence of disbelief because there is still the presence of contradiction.

True wealth only comes to those who not only believe in prosperity consciousness, but who also have empowering thoughts that outweigh and eventually eliminate their disempowering thoughts of limitation and contradiction that are attempting to propel them away from wealth. Thinking in any other way is like adding water to your engine instead of oil. The engine will still perform but it will eventually seize. If you desire that your engine functions to its true and full potential, you must add oil instead of water. Likewise, in order to create and foster abundance in your life, you must add beliefs and thoughts of wealth and abundance and eliminate contradictory beliefs and thoughts of poverty consciousness.

Do you have continuous thoughts related to the attainment of wealth?

Are there more or less contradictory thoughts of poverty consciousness when compared to prosperity consciousness?

Notes:

Date:_____

DELIBERATE THINKING IS DELIBERATELY THINKING YOUR WAY TO SUCCESS

There may be times that we possess discouraging beliefs and thoughts when it appears as though our lives are consistently moving in a negative direction. However, the reason is not because life is deliberately out to get us nor does it result from other's vengeance against us. Unbeknownst to us, it is literally our disempowering beliefs, thoughts and actions that are producing the negative direction in our lives. When we are not mindful of the correlation between our beliefs, thoughts, actions and their subsequent consequences as they relate to our desired experiences, we will not become aware of how they are directly affecting our migration away from our goal.

Whatever is currently occurring in our lives is based directly and indirectly on our current beliefs. Unfortunately, we transfer much, if not all of the old baggage of the past into our current "reality" and, as such, our current "reality" literally becomes a duplication of our past "reality". This is the reason our limiting beliefs and thoughts of the past serve only to limit our lives in the present and future. As thoughts of negativity continue to permeate our minds, the result will be negative actions and thus a negative outcome. Thoughts of negativity will continue to permeate our minds as a result of the negative outcome which, ironically, is based on our habitually negative actions. There is simply no way around this. Negativity in any form in the mind will always produce a negative outcome. We can never go beyond what we currently believe because the limitations we allow to permeate our minds are literally limiting our progress.

However, through the use of mindfulness, we will become aware of how our past beliefs and thoughts have influenced and continue to influence our current beliefs and thoughts. Prior to creating a thought in our minds, we must examine its potential effect on our lives and use this conclusion as a barometer for the re-examination of our current beliefs. How will this thought aid us in our success? What underlying fears are producing these thoughts? How is a lack of belief influencing these thoughts? These are some of the questions that mindfulness fosters. When we analyze our past negative beliefs and thoughts and their associated consequences and compare them to our present beliefs and thoughts, we can almost immediately predict the outcome. If the outcome of our current situation is similar or identical to the outcome of the past, there is a direct correlation between our past and present beliefs.

Since negative beliefs and thoughts produce negative actions and negative actions produce negative experiences, we must intentionally and definitively think thoughts that are deliberate and specific to the creation of what we desire in life. In other words, if a specific outcome is desired, we must believe and think deliberately and specifically in order to achieve this specific outcome. We can deliberately think our way to success through deliberately believing and thinking thoughts related to this success. When we think deliberately, we are seeking to only maintain the types of beliefs and thoughts that are beneficial and will aid our success. Empowering beliefs of success must be consistently introduced into our minds until they habitually produce these deliberate thoughts of success. As these thoughts take a firm hold, they will begin to displace the disempowering thoughts that are permeating our minds.

Deliberate thinking is a process and a way of life in that it will have to be utilized on a daily basis until it becomes habitual. Just like your disempowering thoughts have become habitual as a result of frequent usage, so too can deliberate and intentional positive believing and thinking become habitual.

Are you deliberately believing and thinking thoughts of success?

Which beliefs can you change in order to reprogram your thinking?

Notes:

Date:_____

INTENSIFY YOUR THOUGHTS IN ORDER TO INTENSIFY YOUR LIFE

Throughout this book, I have emphasized how the presence of empowering thoughts affects our actions in a positive manner, while conversely our disempowering thoughts affect our actions in a negative manner. However, there are times when there is a battle for supremacy between the good and the evil; the right and the wrong; the positive thoughts versus the negative thoughts. The result of this pendular battle produces scenarios where you may have positive thoughts at one point and other times the negativity takes over and weighs you down. This pendular conflict subsequently creates conflicting actions that are based on both the negative and the positive thoughts. When this occurs, our actions can be classified as sporadic and chaotic. In one instant we are moving towards our goal and another instant we are moving away from our goal.

Whenever you are intent on progressing towards your goal, but fall victim to self-created thoughts of negativity based on your accepted beliefs of the past or the accepted beliefs of others, you must seek to immediately intensify your positive beliefs. When this is done, you also intensify your positive thoughts and leave little room for the negative thoughts to foster and growth. This allows you to build a secure positive foundation so that it enables you to consistently walk towards your goal without distraction. But how does one intensify their beliefs? You can easily intensify your beliefs by first calming your mind and removing your current frustration and chaos. Thoughts of frustration and chaos are naturally detrimental in nature. If you are intent on reaching your goal, negativity should have no place in your mind. Negativity serves only as a distractor and a destroyer of all things good. The more negative thoughts you have, the further you will travel away from your intended goal due to the frustration and chaos produced in your life as a result of this negativity.

Now that your mind is in a calmer, more relaxing state, locate the source of your disempowering thoughts by using the recapitulation process (Refer to Appendix III). Challenge the premise that first created these thoughts with the intention of eliminating them from your mind. Now you can begin to add new beliefs to strengthen your remaining positive core beliefs by using the belief and possibility matrix (Refer to Appendix IV). When you accept that your desires are not only possible, but are also possible for you and by you, your level of belief and positive thinking will increase. You will intentionally Believe, Think and Achieve your life into fulfillment because you will "know" that success is possible and believe that it is possible for you.

You can also intensify your beliefs and thoughts through the meditation process (Refer to Appendix V). Through this process, you will gradually convince your mind to believe and think in a specific way because "repetition deepens the impression". When you deliberately and continuously think thoughts of success in the present, you build upon previous thoughts of success, until your mind overflows with creative thoughts of success. Not only must you have positive thoughts, but the magnitude and frequency of these thoughts will also affect the outcome. By realizing this little secret, you can intensify your positive beliefs and thoughts so that the outcome of your life can be intensified.

Can you identify areas in your life where an increase in the intensity of your thoughts will prove to be beneficial?

Is your disbelief halting the progress of this increase in intensity?

Notes:

Date:_____

THINK YOUR LIFE INTO FULFILLMENT

Your life, as you currently know it, is based on what you consciously and subconsciously envision in your mind. This vision of yourself affects the thoughts about yourself, others and your interactions with your surroundings. Stop for a second and imagine that the vision that you have of yourself was created on an "erasable canvas". In Principle, what you experience in the "real" world is actually a projection of this image. Thankfully, due to the properties of this "erasable canvas" you, as the artist of your life, can effectively erase and recreate whatever you so desire.

The power of belief is such an amazing tool, but unfortunately, it is either misused or misunderstood. The misuse of the power of belief is highlighted by the majority who desires a life of abundance, but never attains it. There is a desire for a life of abundance, but the vision that is created in their minds is filled with poverty consciousness. Therefore, the life projected from their mental canvas into the "real" world is based on this poverty consciousness. The power of belief is misunderstood in that the negative occurrences of life are seemingly never linked to the negative beliefs that are at the core of its creation. The non-believer is too busy deflecting the blame and never takes the time to establish a relationship between what they believe and what is actually occurring in their lives.

The power of thought is equally powerful because it is

directly based on your beliefs. The very frustration you may be currently experiencing is based on your current beliefs and thoughts. The very happiness that you may be currently experiencing is based on your current beliefs and thoughts. If your life is currently not heading in the direction of fulfillment, then your life is based on your thoughts of lack at the core of your focus. You must first examine your current thoughts and link their effect on your proposed actions. These thoughts will produce the actions which will inevitably take you in the direction of the thought.

If you think in a certain way, you will have certain actions. If you desire fulfillment in your life, you must think fulfilling thoughts. This is the fundamental method of thinking your life into fulfillment. By constantly monitoring these thoughts you can ensure that your actions are optimal. Would you drive to your destination without paying attention to the road signs? If you neglected to do so, you would have no idea if you were speeding or heading in the wrong direction. Likewise, in your travel to fulfillment, you must take notice of not only the types of thoughts you have on a daily basis, but also the frequency of these thoughts.

Once you begin to understand that your current thinking process is based upon your current belief and perception processes, you will seek to alter your beliefs and perceptions so as to alter your thoughts. The old beliefs of poverty consciousness and non-deserving will make way for new and improved thoughts of prosperity consciousness and deserving.

Since everything is based on your perception, a change in your perception will alter the very thing on which you are focused. A perception once based on limitation can only be changed from within. When you have a desire to broaden your perception and follow through with its expansion for the greater good, your subsequent thoughts will no longer be confined to their current limitations. As your beliefs begin to change and your perception is broadened, your subsequent thoughts will follow in accordance. When you mindfully monitor your thoughts, your actions will continue to bring you ever so closer to your life of fulfillment.

What are your current thoughts about your life of fulfillment?

How are your beliefs affecting these thoughts?

Notes:

Date:_____

ACTIONS

LOVE YOURSELF AND OTHERS WILL LOVE YOU TOO

T rue belief is a fundamental power of the universe, but true LOVE is a fundamental power of this belief. Without true love, true positive belief cannot exist. The love we have for ourselves and others creates the belief in ourselves for the greater good; for it is through this greater good that we receive true fulfillment in life. The love of oneself and others always produce a force towards the greater good; for it is this greater good that flows in and around us that propels us towards the essence of true love. Each is related to and dependent on the other.

One of the fundamental beliefs of love stems from our ability to love others as we so love ourselves. But by this very premise, we must first and foremost have love for ourselves before we can even begin to love others. This love that we have for ourselves is not to be mis-categorized with a selfish type of love that may be embraced by many. This love embodies a universal love that is far greater than the love we have for ourselves and others. This universal love symbolizes the power that is inherent in all creation since our universe was created for the enjoyment and love of all humanity. We are simply extracting from this universal love energy to provide the love for ourselves and others.

When we "love" ourselves in a selfish manner, we cannot truly love others because under this selfish philosophy, we are only focusing on ourselves and what we desire 100% of the time. This is a direct contradiction to the universal love, which is based on the nourishment of love for one another and as such a realization of the greater good is never attained. When we love ourselves not in the selfish form of the word, we are allowing ourselves to not only embrace our desires but to also embrace the desires of others as well. This allows all involved to share in the benefits of this universal love by mutual exchange. The type and degree of love that we have for ourselves and others stem from our willingness to embrace the universal love. When we embrace this universal love, we can then have true love for ourselves and others. Our belief in ourselves is a direct correlation to this love.

In order to identify these beliefs about ourselves, we can simply jot down the current thoughts about ourselves on a piece of paper. You would probably be very amazed at what you find. Most, if not all of the beliefs that we have about ourselves stem from our early childhood experiences. These beliefs are either constantly being solidified or are constantly being altered with every experience. Therefore, in order for us to understand why we may not have love for ourselves, we must first examine our current beliefs about ourselves. These beliefs are not only effected by our personal beliefs, but also by the perceived beliefs that we accept from others.

Past situations may have caused us to believe in a certain way and may have affected the love we have for ourselves. But all in all, the amount of love we have for ourselves is actually up to us. We are always free to embrace the true essence of love so that it flows within and permeates through us and draws others to us like a magnet. The amount of love we choose to allow to flow within our lives is also displayed outside of our lives. No one can dictate the amount of love we are allowed to have for ourselves. Unfortunately, we often limit the love we have for ourselves and in ourselves as a result of our limiting beliefs. However, this limited form of "love" does not lend itself to the essence of true love and therefore does not lend itself to the mutual exchange of love from others.

How much love do you currently have for yourself and others?

How can you foster love for yourself and others?

Notes:

Date:_____

CONFIDENCE BUILDS CONFIDENCE

Your very first experience with riding a bicycle probably produced emotions of fear and concern. However, as you became more familiar with the process, your confidence level increased and continued to increase as you became more and more proficient. Eventually, there came a point and time when you were able to ride your bike without any intervention. At this point you were probably completely confident in your ability to ride your bike and other types of bikes as well. This scenario appropriately describes how the initial introduction to an unknown appears to be insurmountable, but gradually becomes easier and more manageable as you become acclimated.

Whenever you are faced with an entirely new situation or a needed change in your life, you may be afraid if not petrified at first. However, as you begin to embrace this change, your fear will begin to diminish and make way for increased confidence. This simple principle can be applied to every aspect of your life. The new business you are contemplating; that new house or new job you desire all may seem insurmountable at first. However, the very first step you take, like riding a bicycle, will add the confidence necessary to build further confidence.

Your mind possesses a powerful method of assimilating you to your environment. For instance, a weight lifter gradually gains muscle as he or she practices; so do the mental capacities of your mind increase as you utilize its abilities. Familiarity by its very nature produces even more familiarity as a result of exposure. However, when you allow yourself to become stagnant and complacent, you are not engaging in the familiarity building process, but you are actually retreating from it. The more you retreat from exposing yourself to becoming familiar with the process you desire to master, the more likely you will never produce enough confidence to master the experience.

The pivotal point of any exposure is the initial step in your mind!

Prior to engaging in the initial step in your mind, all of your old fears of the past will flow in to produce your fears of the present, consequently paralyzing your thoughts and actions. It may seem as though you have to muster up enough energy just to engage in this step even though you realize that your subsequent steps will become progressively easier. In principle, when you believe that you will have future negative experiences, this belief will affect your subsequent thoughts in the present. This disbelief in your ability will foster thoughts that are destructive to your ability to build and maintain confidence. Furthermore, your choices and your subsequent actions will indicate a lack of confidence in anything that you do or say.

In order to build and maintain confidence prior to making that first initial step, you must alter your current belief system to include a belief that the journey you are about to embark on is not only absolutely possible, but it is absolutely possible by you. Even if you do not possess the expertise to get the job done, you know that you have other alternatives available and the job will get done. When you embrace this change in your belief system, the very first physical step you take will prove to be much easier than you ever imagined.

Which areas are you lacking in confidence?

How can you take the first step in your mind through the inclusion of your beliefs?

Notes:

Date:_____

A LACK OF BELIEF PRODUCES A LACK OF ACTION

W hen you do not believe, you are subsequently fearful and therefore you do not attempt to achieve your desires. You are literally living in fear and adding resistance to the receipt of all that you desire to receive. You are not exercising your capability to believe nor are you willing to exercise your capability to believe in your ability to create an outcome according to the way you desire. Your lack of belief and its associated fears literally preserve you in a perpetual state of paralysis. You simply cannot seem to move. Ironically, this lack of belief and its associated paralysis have very little to do with your actual ability to take action. In fact you may be very well positioned to take action and leap into success, but until you believe and perceive it as such, your actions will indicate otherwise.

Belief is actually a two-fold question directed at (1) the overall possibility of success and (2) the possibility of individualized success. Thus, the first question, "Is what I desire possible?" relates to your belief in the overall possibility, while the second question, "Is my desire possible for me?" relates to the possibility of success for you (Refer to Appendix IV). You may literally believe that your desires are possible because you have observed the success of others, but if you do not believe that the same or greater success is possible for you, you will take no further action. There are many elements of your psychology that may prohibit the realization of your individual success. Your past limiting beliefs, social and experiential conditioning, thoughts of non-deserving and even a fear of success will offer resistance to the realization of your individual success.

Typically, when you observe others who have attained a level of success or the things that you desire, an all too common mistake is to either presume that they were "lucky" in the attainment of their desires or to evoke jealousy towards them. However, to admit that their beliefs, thoughts and actions justified their receipt of success would be a direct reflection on your ability to do likewise. This would imply that your current situation is actually a direct and indirect result of your choice to believe, think and act in a specific way that is offering resistance to the receipt of your goals. Therefore, in an attempt to camouflage your own self-created deficiencies, you dub their attainment of success as pure luck.

A life based on fear is a life based on disbelief. You cannot eliminate the fear when you do not believe and you cannot truly believe until you eliminate the fear. In order for you to have true success and fulfillment, both cannot coexist in the same space. You must eliminate the fear by believing not only in the achievability of your vision of success, but also in the tangibility of this vision as it directly applies to you (Refer to Appendix IV). When you create a vision of success in your mind, what do you have to be afraid of if you believe in this vision? By first creating a vision of your success, you will become the author and the inspiration for everything that occurs in your life. However, before you can create a vision of your success, you must be willing to focus intently on this vision until it becomes your reality. This is one of the key ways that you can increase your level of belief in your vision. Think about your vision on a daily basis; in the morning; driving to and from work; while at work; when you are at the grocery store and before you go to bed at night. Have it constantly on your mind; your core point of focus will eventually become your reality.

You must gladly focus with intent on your vision; knowing that by doing so, you will convert the images in your mind into your actual reality. The more you participate in the creation of the specifics of this vision of success, the more you will begin to build an "intimate relationship" with this vision. You cannot simply focus on your vision of success for a short period of time and expect it to materialize. Similar to any other habit, you must consistently repeat the process in order for it to take a foothold in your life. The fearful emotions associated with change and disbelief will gradually dissipate as you intimately experience this vision of your success on a daily basis.

You have already created a vision in your mind that is not entirely based on your success; therefore you must build a habitual experience with your new vision based on your ultimate success. Remember, you may start with good intentions, but it will quickly fade if your focus is not fixated intently on your ultimate vision of success. By intentionally believing and subsequently thinking thoughts related to your success, you can jumpstart and propel the process of reprogramming your current beliefs and thoughts. Remember, the process of reprogramming your mind is tantamount to breaking an old habit. You must be mindful, vigilant and committed at all times for the process to work effectively.

Do you have a vision of success but a lack of action to-wards this vision of success?

How can you jumpstart your belief in your personal ability to attain this success?

Notes:

Date:_____

ACCEPTING WHAT LIFE HAS DEALT YOU IS ACCEPTING A LIFE WITHOUT FULFILLMENT

I have heard many people state that life has dealt them a particular hand; they have no choice but to deal with what they were "dealt". This is so far from the truth because in actuality, it was the choices that they made in the past that created the current obstacles in the present. They also do not realize that the choices that are made from this point forward will further define their life in the future. By no means do we go through life solely accepting what life has "dealt" us. We actually go through life creating the experiences of life based on our beliefs and choices. For example, even a choice to do nothing is still a choice; we will have to interact with the consequences of this choice. We are not accepting what life has "dealt" us but instead are creating what life has dealt us.

Whatever our current situation may be, we _**always**_ have a choice in the matter. The choices that we currently perceive do not preclude the existence of other alternative choices beyond our current scope of perception. Unfortunately, the choices that we typically perceive do not include the available alternative choices because they are beyond our current scope of perception.

When our perceived available choices appear to be less than desirable, frustration in our current situation is typically the outcome. It appears as though our available choices are extremely limited and we are forced to accept "what life has dealt us". The irony resides in the fact that the very frustration that we feel is further limiting our perception and consequently resulting in additional frustration. Even though the frustration that we feel is restricting our view and ability to recognize all of the other alternatives available to us, there are _always_ available choices beyond our currently perceived limited choices. We are not the first to be entangled in this web and we most certainly will not be the last. How have others resolved the very situation that we are going through? There is _always_ a way out. The choice must be made to clear our minds of fear and frustration and expand our belief to include the attainment of our ultimate success, even in the face of adversity.

In order to break out of the mold and create a new life according to our desires, we must challenge the very core notion of the saying "what life has dealt us". We must dig deep within ourselves and create a burning desire for a life of fulfillment! If we accepted "what life has dealt us", we are accepting a life based on an acceptance of limiting beliefs. We have the power to decide what we desire in life. We have the ability to locate or create solutions to our "problems". Calm the mind by removing the frustrating and chaotic thoughts through the process of intentionally believing (Refer to Appendix IV). This will clear the path that will enable the answers to flow quickly and effortlessly.

Any time we accept "what life has dealt us", we are relinquishing our ability to directly control our life and destiny with intent. Even when it appears as though our life is out of control, this mechanistic view of a lack of control must be challenged. "It is what it is" is simply a perception. If we change our perception, it will render a change in our current situation. This change in perception will also affect all of our future outcomes. If we desire a life of fulfillment, we MUST take charge of our lives in every aspect and not allow our destructive and limiting thoughts to dictate our course of action. This can only be accomplished through the eradication of the limiting beliefs that are driving our thoughts of limitation. When we expand our beliefs to include our ultimate success, we will then be able to sit at the table and enjoy a five course meal and not fight for the crumbs that have fallen from the table.

Do you believe that you are at the mercy of life?

If so, how can a change in this belief create a change in perception in order to create a change in your life?

Notes:

Date:_____

OBSTACLES IN THE MIND LEAD TO OBSTACLES UNDER YOUR FEET

O bstacles in your path to success do not always represent physical limitations such as abilities, insufficient money or time. In fact, these so called physical obstacles in the "real" world are but a manifestation of the mental obstacles that permeate from your mind. Therefore, since it is your beliefs and thoughts that construct your experiences in the "real" world, it only stands true that any type of mental obstacle such as contradictory and limiting beliefs and thoughts will automatically produce physical obstacles in your life. These mental obstacles are merely a perception of what you believe is possible or impossible in your life. The perception of obstacles in one's life is solely based on the mechanistic view of obstacles in the mind. You decide which obstacles, if any, are present in your mind and thus in your life. It is entirely within your reach to eliminate the mental obstacles in your mind so as to eliminate the obstacles in your life. It is all a matter of perception! Thus, a perceived obstacle by one person may be another person's source of opportunity.

There are certain things in your life that are absolute. For example, the last time you checked your bank account, you only had $25 available and this certainly will not buy that new living room set you always desired. But if you viewed the $25 as a perceived lack and you continued to focus on this mechanistic view of lack, you will never receive that living room set you always desired. The living room set cost $1,000, however the "problem" is that you currently only have $25 available in your bank account. The natural tendency is to focus on the fact that you do not have enough to make the purchase. If you had a "real" job or if you were as good as your other siblings, you would be able to afford this nice living room set, you surmise. Unfortunately, this mode of thinking is a classic example of a focus that is exclusively on the "problem" and not on the solution.

However, by calming your mind and focusing on solutions, your thoughts will begin to be different. For example, if the current job does not provide sufficient income for you, what can you do to increase it? Analyze the actions of your friends, family and peers in order to ascertain which beliefs brought them to this point in their lives. Which good points from their lives can you add to your own life? Taken from another perspective, this may actually be an opportunity for you and may propel you to initiate a change in career or finally start that business you were contemplating for years. When you believe as though you have already received your lovely living room set and you are truly committed to this belief, you will calmly and relentlessly search for the answers, knowing that you will receive them. The answers are all around you!

Whenever you place obstacles in your mind by your thoughts of disbelief, non-deserving or not being good enough, you are creating giant obstacles and placing them directly in your path. Whatever limiting and contradictory thoughts you have of yourself; whatever obstacles you perceive that you had in the past and will continue to have in the future are only feeding and contributing to your present disempowering beliefs, thoughts and actions. A reliance on the negativity of the past and the present as a predictor for the future will cause you to become complacent in the present. For example, if you perceive that the obstacles of the past will continue in the future, your actions in the present WILL be those of complacency towards building a future that is different from the past. Therefore, focusing on your past "obstacles" and any perceived future "obstacles" will eventually bring about exactly what you envision; a life that is identical to your perception.

What obstacles are you creating in your mind?

How will your life improve by the removal of these mental obstacles?

Notes:

Date:_____

THE BEST WAY TO DEVELOP GOOD HABITS IS TO STAY AWAY FROM BAD HABITS

Habits are generally developed as a result of a continuous process involving the habit. A bad habit is developed as a result of a continuous association with the bad habit in question, whereas a good habit is developed from a continuous association with the good habit in question. However, the development of a habit does not necessarily require repeated exposure over an extended period of time but may be developed as a result of an initial introduction to the act. If a high enough value is placed on the act, the act itself may become immediately intertwined with your pattern of behavior, thus developing a destructive or constructive behavioral pattern.

When you are mindful of your thoughts and emotions, you are also mindful of your current situation and the situations in which you place yourself on a daily basis. When you are focused on arriving at your goal in the manner that YOU prescribe, you must guard well the avenues to the decision process that affects your actions. This decision process is directly affected by what you believe; what you perceive based on these beliefs and a conclusive believe based on the combination of the two. When these avenues are mindfully guarded, you are ensuring that only good information is fed into your mental database. This is analogous to a computer system where garbage in produces garbage out. The same effect holds true with your decision making process.

If you expose your mind to negativity, disbelief, non-deserving and fear based thoughts; you are setting up yourself for a diversion from your true potential and also establishing yourself for the continuous receipt of the same. You must be cautious about what you believe and perceive because whatever you believe and perceive is what you will receive in your life. The habits that you develop as a result of what you believe and perceive will affect you not only in the present but also in the future.

A sure way to develop good habits in the first place is to stay away from habits that you know are destructive. Even if you initially do not recognize the detrimental attributes of the habit, you should still analyze it and decide on whether or not to continue based on its ability to get you to your goal. If this habit produces experiences and circumstances that bring you closer to your goal, clearly it is a habit that is worth adopting. On the other hand, if the opposite occurs, clearly it is a habit that you must immediately neglect. Negative thinking of any kind is an example of such a habit that you must immediately neglect.

What destructive habits do you currently have?

What immediate steps are you taking to eradicate these habits?

Notes:

Date:_____

THE POWER OF CHOICE IS VERY DIFFERENT FROM THE ABILITY TO CHOOSE

We are endowed with the ability to choose. The Creator granted us this great privilege and ability in order for us to freely choose the course of our lives. But the ability to choose does not automatically create great power in our lives. The real power resides in the types of choices we make and not simply in our ability to choose. For example, even an individual who commits suicide has the ability to choose; the choice was to commit suicide. Simply because we possess the ability to choose does not render it factual that we will automatically make the choices that produce the most power. Each of our choices carries with it a potentially negative or positive end result. In Principle, the result of our lives is not hinged upon our ability to choose but rather on the election of either a negatively destructive choice or a positively empowering choice.

We are aware that we have the ability to choose, but do we actually believe that there is an immense power associated with each of our choices? Of course not! If this were true, the world would be a much better place as a result of a much better life for each of us. We perceive that we are free to choose our destiny because we have the ability to freely choose, but what we do not realize is that simply relying on the ability to freely choose without regard to the ultimate consequences of our choices is actually enslaving our lives and removing all traces of freedom.

Most of us do not realize the power contained in our choices, otherwise we would certainly be much more selective of our choices. We often make choices based on instant gratification while choosing to ignore the potentially negative outcome of these choices. If we choose to make a choice based on instant gratification while ignoring the potential consequences, we are exercising our ability to choose but we are not diligently selecting the choice with the most power. When we are tempted to make a decision based on instant gratification, we must analyze the potential consequences of this decision and compare it to our desired outcome. When we are tempted to be complacent, we must analyze the power inherent in <u>ALL</u> of our available alternatives and choose the one/s that produces the best benefit for our lives, regardless of our desire for instant gratification.

Selecting the choices with the most power signifies a mindful interaction with the choices **we choose to perceive** are available. It is important to note that available choices signify a meaning that is very different from perceived choices; one relates to choices that are actually available while the other relates to choices that have been filtered and limited by our limiting beliefs respectively. If the choices we perceive are available promote a life that is in opposition to our desires, we <u>MUST</u> change our perception. This will reveal an entire array of available choices not seen previously under the old mechanistic view.

We have the ability to choose what we wear, eat, drink, the type of car or home we purchase and so on however, this is typically the extent of our involvement in our ability to choose. If we examined this further, we would conclude that our ability to choose what to wear, eat and drink is only a microscopic part of the equation. However, when we make choices such as choosing to wear clothes that make us feel successful; eating foods that are healthy for us or refraining from activities that are destructive, we are not just exercising our ability to choose, but we are making powerful productive choices. The remaining elements of the equation however include the choices relative to the types of beliefs, thoughts and actions we choose to create and allow to perpetuate our lives.

Are your beliefs, thoughts and actions limiting your true potential and offering resistance to the attainment of self-actualization and self-fulfillment? Do you live your life limited by a set of limiting perceptions? These are some of the questions that imply an ability to choose but require choices based on the promotion of powerful choices. Whenever you analyze your current situation with calmness and mindfulness, you are far better equipped to create fulfillment in your life through the election of powerful choices.

Powerful life changes come when we use our ability to choose to make powerful choices. Each choice that we make is an exercise in underscoring what we believe. Even the simplest of choices is an indication of this belief. For example, the simple choice to purchase a particular bottle of detergent relates to our belief in the detergent's ability to clean our clothes relative to our perceived ability to purchase the detergent. A decision to purchase a particular type of car or home is also related to our belief in what these things will provide for us and our belief in our ability to pay for these things. We would not buy a bottle of detergent if we did not believe that it would clean our clothes nor would we purchase a beautiful car if we believed that it would leave us stranded on the highway.

Everything we think, say or do has its roots buried in what we believe. But we are typically not conditioned to analyze the reasons for our thoughts and actions as it relates to what we actually believe. Imagine if we were to evaluate our thoughts and actions to ascertain the core beliefs that are literally driving these thoughts and actions. The revelation would probably be astounding. We would probably uncover destructive beliefs about ourselves that we never knew existed. The power inherent in conducting such an analysis is correlated to a desire to first recognize our destructive beliefs and subsequently taking steps to eradicate or alter these beliefs. This is the beauty of mindfulness.

We engage in numerous choices every day; some consciously intentional and some consciously unintentional but subconsciously intentional. But it is not our ability to choose that brings about a powerful change in our lives; it is the power of our choices based on what you belief is possible. Yes, we do have the ability to choose, but we also have the ability to choose to do the wrong things whether intentionally or unintentionally. Either way, it is still a choice that we have elected to make.

When we make powerful choices and maintain commitment to these choices, our life will change in a powerful way. These powerful choices are made possible not by our ability to recognize that we are free to choose, but by the recognition that our choices have the power to affect our life in either a positive or negative way. When we use our ability to choose to make choices that are questionable, we are deciding not to believe in our ability to create our life according to our specifications. When we believe in our ability to create our life to our specifications, the choices that we make will be those that will continually seek to maximize our possibilities at all times.

Since we all have the ability to choose, it is up to us to choose how we will exercise this ability. If we fall victim to instant gratification, complacency, complaining and frustration, we are still actively making choices, albeit destructive choices that we have decided to accept. Frustration simply does not come from non-interaction; it comes as a result of a choice to accept the perceived limitations of our current situation. However, when we are engaged in mindfulness, we will realize that there are always alternative choices available. When we calm our minds and focus intently on the solution and not the "problem", we will not make choices that are hasty, fearful or chaotic.

We must also recognize that with every choice, there is a consequence based on the choice itself. When we make decisions that are fear based, we will eventually suffer the consequences of our hasty and chaotic decisions. However, when we make choices based on knowing and believing that our future will be bright, we are choosing to make choices that are extremely powerful.

Do you deliberate the potential consequences of <u>ALL</u> of your choices?

How often do you attempt to uncover the beliefs that are driving these choices?

Notes:

Date:_____

PERSONAL POWER IS THE POWER THAT YOU POSSESS WITHIN YOU THAT CAN PRODUCE A LIFE CHANGING EXPERIENCE WITHIN AND WITHOUT

The meaning of personal power is exactly that; a powerful personal ability that you possess within you that contains the element of empowerment to produce a change within you, resulting in a change around you. Even though you may not be currently aware of its existence, you still possess a certain level of personal power. The level of personal power that you possess is determined by none other than you. You have control over the magnitude of your personal power simply by the beliefs that you give to it. The greater the beliefs and the greater the dedication to these beliefs, the greater the output of your personal power potential and the greater the life changing experience within you which will subsequently produce a life changing experience around you.

You have the potential for greatness! This greatness is realized through focusing on the correct mix of attributes that are ultimately designed to accentuate your inner personal power potential. Some of these attributes include belief, tenacity, commitment, perseverance, mindfulness and so on. The recipe necessary to harness this power will vary from individual to individual but the ingredients are all the same. All in all, the extent of the benefits received from your personal power will depend on the correct recipe or mixture of these ingredients.

The exact level of these ingredients will vary from individual to individual; some will have a greater level of one element than others. However, the ultimate effect can still be the same; a life changing experience for the greater good. You may inherently have certain abilities that have been developed over time that will enable you to capitalize on your personal power potential at a quicker rate than others. On the other hand, you may not have consciously developed such traits and subsequently will have to take the time necessary to foster its growth in your life. All in all, your achievement of a life changing experience hinges on your commitment to create and believe in our vision of success as opposed to struggling with the idea and concept. Until you are at the point of mastery, there will be a trial and error process involved in the engagement of the key ingredients to your personal power. Use each misstep to fine-tune each of your subsequent process until proficiency is achieved.

Personal power is initialized when you truly believe in the possibility of a change in your life; you believe in your ability to make such a change and you are truly committed to this change. A final decision to bring about this change will occur as soon as you solidify your total belief in a change for the better in your life. By engaging in this initial process, you are making an immutable affirmation. Your beliefs will invigorate your thoughts and your invigorated thoughts will energize your subsequent actions. Your commitment will enable you to monitor and adjust your thoughts, emotions and actions to ensure that you remain on track. In short, the key ingredients for the initiation and development of your personal power are belief, commitment, decision and action; the success of which hinges upon the continuity in each.

Do you possess the key elements of person power?

_____

_____

If not, how can you incorporate the missing elements into your life?

_____

_____

Notes:

_____

_____

_____

_____

_____

_____

Date:_____

PERSONAL SUCCESS IS NOT A MATTER OF CHANCE...IT IS A MATTER OF CREATION, MANAGED EMOTIONS, FOCUSED INTENTION AND DELIBERATE ACTION

I n order for you to have personal success and fulfillment in your life you must first create a specific vision of your personal success and fulfillment in your mind. This vision must specifically include what you desire; from the detailed style of your desired home to the exact color and type of car that you desire. The more details you can add to this vision, the more real this vision will become to you. Many of us have a vision of our desired life of success; however this vision is relatively vague and is lacking the specifics that are needed to elucidate this vision. If you cannot see the style, color, location and size of the home that you desire to live in, then how can you realize this desire? If you cannot envision the specifics of your desired lifestyle, then how can you achieve it? If you envision a generic lifestyle without incorporating the specifics that you desire, your vision of success will not be filled with clarity but with illusions and shadows.

You can only achieve what you are willing to envision and believe! A vision that is opaque does not command the intensity of focus as does a vision that is lucid. It is the intensity of your focus that literally promotes the creation of the focus of your thoughts. Your beliefs, thoughts, emotions and actions all play an integral role in your personal success and fulfillment.

╫ Mindfulness in its true form is the constant awareness and management of these beliefs, thoughts, emotions and actions as they relate to your ability to achieve your desired goal.

╫ Mindfulness not only monitors the types of thoughts and emotions that you have, but it also monitors every aspect of these thoughts and emotions, starting from their point of inception to the actual decisions that result from these thoughts and emotions.

╫ Mindfulness enables you to monitor your beliefs, thoughts and your actions while your focus determines the types of beliefs, thoughts and actions that are introduced and maintained in your mind.

╫ Mindfulness in concert with focus is what empowers you to remain on the correct path at all times towards the intentions of your goal.

In the absence of focused intentions, you will easily wander off the path towards your goal without arriving at this conclusive realization. The types of thoughts you have on a consistent basis is always relative to the direction of your focus. If you desire a life of success, but allow your focus to be skewed by negativity, your life will be misdirected towards negativity. You make it increasingly difficult for yourself to achieve your life of success when your focus is on the negative as opposed to the positive. The caveat is that your actions will be deliberate regardless of whether your thoughts are negative or positive. Negative thoughts will produce negative deliberate and destructive actions, whereas positive thoughts will produce positive deliberate constructive actions. In Principle, when your thoughts are positively based, your actions will become positively deliberate and will deliberately propel you towards your goal of a life of abundance.

Do you currently have negative limiting beliefs that are disrupting your thoughts?

Are you prepared to engage in a bit of self-analysis in order to identify these beliefs?

Notes:

Date:_____

ARRIVING AT YOUR DESTINATION INVOLVES FOLLOWING A PRESCRIBED ROUTE

This sounds simple enough, right? You know exactly where you desire to go and you know how to get there; or do you? There are many ways to arrive at your destination. It all depends on which route you choose and how you view the situations that occur while traveling on your route to your destination. If you desire to get from point A to point B using the shortest route possible, but the directions were not known to you, you would typically consult a map for directions to point B. If point B is located north of point A, clearly, in order to arrive expeditiously at point B, you would not travel south of point A. This action would lead you in a totally different direction and therefore a totally different destination. If you desire to arrive at point B in the shortest possible time from your original starting point of A, you must follow a prescribed route based on your intention of arriving as quickly as possible. If time was not a concern, then of course you can select the longer scenic route. But since time is a concern, you would probably fare better by selecting the shortest route possible.

This scenario applies to all of the decisions that you make in life. When you have a particular goal in mind, the path that you choose must be specifically designed with the final intentions of your goal in mind. However, when you choose a path that is not specifically designed for your goal, you are not considering the final intentions of your goal and you may be delayed at arriving at your goal or you may end up at another destination altogether. Your path must be in line with your intentions, that is, if you desire to arrive at your goal within a particular time frame, the path that you choose must also take this into consideration, otherwise you will arrive at our goal but not based on your intentions.

Everything in life is based on the power of belief and everything in life has a consequence, whether good or bad, that is related to the use of this power of belief. Whatever you believe will create the negative or positive experiences in your life. Therefore, if your desire is to welcome specific results in your life, you must participate in specific types of beliefs, thoughts and actions. If you desire to arrive at a specific destination in life, you must take a specific route. As you travel along the path to your goal, you must use any situation that offers frustration and resistance as measurable feedback to ensure that you are able to fine-tune your beliefs, thoughts and actions. When you use this feedback to your benefit, you are functioning like a Global Positioning System (GPS) system, which allows you to recalculate your current beliefs so that you can get back on the correct route to your goal.

Which route have you chosen based on your intentions?

What beliefs have affected the route you have chosen?

Notes:

Date:_____

YOU WILL NEVER ARRIVE AT YOUR GOAL IF YOU ARE MOVING AWAY FROM YOUR GOAL

S it back and think about this statement over a nice cup of coffee every day for about a week. You will probably be amazed at what you find. A simple saying such as this seems quite intuitive in its implications, but as you dig deeper into its fundamentals, you will realize that we are all culprits of violating this simple truth. Many analogies have been made regarding this premise but the true essence of the statement resides in your understanding and belief in this statement. For examples, if you desire to walk from your present location to a particular destination, you have to at least place one foot in front of the other in order to move forward. Additionally, the steps that you take must be in the direction of your destination, otherwise you will not arrive at your destination. However, the simplicity of this statement often highlights the many complexities in life.

In order to travel from your current position of point A to your desired position of point B, you must practice the beliefs, thoughts and actions that are specific to the arrival at point B. The steps taken must be in the direction of point B otherwise the only movement that will be experienced is movement that is away from the goal of point B. If your destination is positive, you cannot practice negative, contradictory and limiting beliefs, thoughts and actions while expecting to arrive at your destination. You are the creator of your life and as such you are in control of the direction of your life. For example, when you decide to sit idly by in complacency and despair, you will not see positive movement in your life. You have the ability to choose your own destination and you also have the ability to choose your next course of action towards the destination you have chosen.

If you choose a particular destination in your mind, the only way that you are actually going to arrive at your destination is through movement towards that destination both in your mind and in your actions. In order for there to be constant movement towards your goal, there must be constant movement from within you. In order for there to be constant movement towards your goal, there must not be constant movement away from your goal.

No one else is to blame for either your chosen lack of movement or your chosen movement in a direction that is in opposition to your desires. You are in control of your movement even when you choose to become complacent and deflect the blame for your lack of movement onto someone or something. When you indicate that you have done the best that you could based on the circumstances, you are making a decision to refrain from continuously seeking other alternatives while refusing to acknowledge the part you are playing in the construction of your circumstances. When you are willing to continuously seek other alternatives, you will expand your efforts and maintain your momentum as a result of a commitment to your belief. Without true commitment, you will quickly become complacent and refrain from generating the essential movement towards your goal. Limiting beliefs actually limits your life. Identify them and begin to alter these beliefs so that your direction is no longer in opposition to your goal.

Are you currently moving towards or away from your goal?

Are your goals stagnated because of complacency?

Notes:

Date:_____

HAPPINESS COMES AS A RESULT OF DELIBERATING ONE'S THOUGHTS BEFORE ONE'S ACTIONS

Most people enjoy the results of a positive situation. No "logical" person would deliberately place themself in a situation that would bring unhappiness into their lives. In principle, the pursuit of happiness is a fundamental impetus for our continued existence. However, it is imperative to note that what may make one person happy may be detrimental to another and vice versa. Happiness, as defined by conventional terms, is not an objective truth, but rather it is both subjective and relative; therefore it is based on a perception. Your perception of happiness hinges upon what you define as fulfilling and satisfying in your life. For example, a beggar may be happy living on the streets whereas most of us cannot even bear the thought of doing so.

Our words and our actions are a direct result of our conscious and subconscious beliefs and thoughts. Since our actions are directly related to these conscious and subconscious beliefs and thoughts, it suggests that we must continuously deliberate our beliefs, thoughts and emotions to ensure that the resulting actions will not directly or indirectly produce an undesirable outcome. When our actions produce an undesirable outcome, this negative outcome can alter our current beliefs through the acceptance of certain negative principles based on this outcome. Thus, this outcome will serve to create additional thoughts that are also negative, which in turn reciprocate by producing further negative actions and outcomes. Through the use of mindfulness, these undesirable outcomes can be examined for clues that highlight the necessary changes that can promote future positive outcomes.

The correct pursuit of happiness is a lifestyle that is based on exercising one's ability to compare proposed actions with the actions that are required for the attainment of happiness. All too often, we elect instant gratification at the expense of future lifelong happiness. But since there is a cause and effect relationship inherent in everything that we do, the effect of a life of happiness must be derived from the correct cause. Complainers are notorious for indulging in activities that produce and reproduce undesirable effects. They do not embrace the mindful lifestyle of deliberating their thoughts before their actions and therefore do not realize how their beliefs are actually affecting and controlling their actions. They complain that they are never quite able to "get a break" in life because they perceive that their negative experiences are happening TO them. They have no awareness or they do not desire to possess an awareness of how their undeliberated thoughts are actually creating the very things they complain about.

When we choose to integrate deliberation into our daily diet, we are strategically planning for our success. We are able to simulate the influences that our beliefs and thoughts will have on our proposed actions and preemptively make the necessary changes prior to engaging in potentially destructive behavior. Instead of selecting an action randomly or based on undeliberated emotions, we will select only those actions that are required for the acquisition of our desired goal; the outcome of which will produce the fruit necessary for our lives of abundance.

Are you currently happy with the direction of your life?

How are your beliefs, thoughts and actions affecting this direction?

Notes:

Date:_____

SUCCESS IS FINDING A WAY TO MAKE POSSIBLE YOUR "IMPOSSIBILITIES"

If Thomas Edison or any of the countless innovators had given up in the face of adversity, can you imagine where we would be now? What would life be without electricity, the light bulb, television, computers and so on? The answer to this question is one I know we would much rather ignore. But it was through their continued efforts in the face of adversity that made the seemingly impossible tasks possible. There was an unquestionable belief and commitment on their part that provided them with the tenacity to persevere in the face of their adversities.

Life is no different. Even if it takes 10,000 tries to make possible your perceived "impossibilities", the most important point is to remain focused and committed to your beliefs. Your commitment level to what you truly believe will define the course of action you will take and continue to take. A vision of your success without a strong belief in this success will render your vision null and void. Thus, your dreams and aspirations will not be realized or only marginally realized. It is your strong belief in your success that gives your vision and your life true meaning and purpose. I cannot completely stress the importance of your beliefs. Any amount of disbelief will wreak havoc on your ability to achieve your desired success.

Making possible your perceived "impossibilities" is tantamount to redefining your current life from where it is now to where you choose to take it in the future. The only thing that is causing you to perceive impossibilities in your life are your core beliefs. These core beliefs are the driving force that can either produce limitations or promote expansion in your way of thinking. However, these core beliefs are not absolute since they can be changed at any time. Just because you have held onto these old beliefs for most of your life does not conclude that you cannot eradicate them from your mind. Your life of success and abundance highly depends on your decision to believe that you will achieve a life of success and abundance. When you choose to believe that you do not deserve a life of abundance or that it is not possible, you are setting yourself up for the creation of failure.

The failure that is created in your life results from the types of thoughts you are currently thinking. These thoughts that promote failure as a created option will cause you to make choices that will inevitably produce "impossibilities" in your life; thus producing the very "failures" that you were focusing on. However, there are always multiple solutions to your perceived "impossibilities" and there are also multiple ways to locate or create these solutions.

Typically, the recognition of alternatives that are already available is marred by our inherent fear of change. But remember, any change that has the potential to produce goodness in your life is always a good change and must be embraced regardless of your fear of this change. Even if you do not currently recognize alternatives or do not look favorably on the ones you do recognize, because of your own inhibitions and fears, they are still alternative solutions readily waiting to be harvested. You can consult the expertise of others who have gone through or are currently going through what you are experiencing or you can engage in external research yourself.

The creative juices will flow when and only when your mind is calm and free of frustration. The largest restrictor of creative thought is fear. It paralyses and restricts your view of possibilities, while only revealing that which you fear. However, when you believe that your success is absolutely possible and is also possible for you, your level of fear will gradually diminish and disappear, making way for the recognition of possibilities in your life. You just have to take the initial step and maintain the positive momentum until you reach your goal.

What perceived "impossibilities" are you current facing?

How can brainstorming to consider ALL options that are outside of your comfort zone aid you in locating or creating alternatives?

Notes:

Date:_____

WHERE THERE IS A WILL THERE IS A WAY, BUT WHERE THERE IS NO WILL THERE IS NO WAY

Plain and simple, if we absolutely desire to or are required to get something accomplished, we will find a way. Even if we have to sacrifice something of greater or lesser value of importance, our desire will provide us with the necessary energy, time and resources, provided that we continue to believe in the possibility of its attainment. Nothing will stand in our way because our desire is fixated on the accomplishment of the task at hand. For example, if it takes all night to complete a task that is due in the morning, we will typically allocate the necessary resources as long as we continue to believe that it can be accomplished by morning. In other words, when there is continued belief in the possibility of an accomplishment, the necessary resources WILL be allocated and action WILL be taken to complete the task. However, when there is disbelief, the necessary resources are illusive and no action will be taken. Thus the task will not be started, much less completed.

But why do we dedicate our precious resources of time and money to complete a physical task, but cannot dedicate the same resources to the initiation and completion of a productive change in our lives? The answer stems from our belief in what we perceive is possible and attainable. For example, we believe that it is mandatory to stay awake all night to complete a report that is due in the morning because we would rather lose a good night sleep, rather than face the wrath of our employer. Ironically, why is the same amount of determination and commitment to affect a change absent in our lives? The primary difference resides in the fact that our employers mandate an immediate response, whereas we do not perceive the future detrimental effects in our lives from a lack of immediate response. In the grand scheme of our lives, we will eventually not be accountable to an employer, but we will be accountable to ourselves.

In order to increase the level of commitment, we must truly believe in our success and absolutely decide within ourselves, without question, what we desire. By making an absolute decision to believe, we initiate a chain of thoughts and actions that set about motion powered by sheer determination. Nothing will stand in our way because we have already decided that our commitment and determination will win over all obstacles.

However, when there is no absolute decision to believe, we are allowing our thoughts and actions to be dictated by means other than what is required for the attainment of our desires. We may or may not reach our goal depending on the amount of determination we have at that particular moment. The likelihood of this occurring depends on the probability of the right mix of belief, thoughts and actions as opposed to the deliberate use of our creative abilities to evoke the correct mix that will absolutely get us to our goal.

When there is no absolute belief and resolve, excuses become our mantra. The presence of disbelief in our abilities typically produces these excuses, while causing us to subsequently transfer the blame for our situation onto someone or something. We see no way out of our current situation and eventually become comfortable in our complacency. We perceive that it is simply easier to complain rather than foster and ignite our will power into achieving what we desire. If we only knew the harm that we are bringing upon ourselves through the complaining process, we would literally staple our mouths closed so that we could not utter a single word.

All too often we give way to beliefs, thoughts and actions that dampen our will power. These limiting beliefs, thoughts and actions eat away at our core and drastically weaken our will power, especially if we were not initially 100% dedicated. Without this will power delivering the needed energy reserves to continue, we will quickly give up and return to our old habitual ways of limiting beliefs, limiting thoughts, limiting actions and a limited life. Remember, in order to produce a change, we have to abandon our disempowering way of believing and thinking.

There is extreme will power potential within us all! The critical element is whether we believe in its existence and subsequently decide to utilize it. Sure, it takes physical and mental mindfulness to build momentum in our lives, but the end result will more than compensate for the changes made. In actuality, our engagement in mindfulness must not be looked upon as a sacrifice, because every thought and action that that leads us closer to our goal deserves a celebratory standing ovation.

Do you believe that a change is possible in your life?

Do you have the desire necessary to effect this change in your life?

Notes:

Date:_____

LIVING WITH TRUE PURPOSE IS LIFE LIVED PURPOSELY

L ife must explicitly be about living with intent. Living with intent is about living with a strong sense of purpose. When we live our lives without fulfillment, we are not capitalizing on the full advantage of all that is available. However, when we live our lives with intent, there is a definite purpose and direction. We will not drift aimlessly in the sea of life, but instead, chart a direct course towards our destination, while we cruise there straight and true.

Unfortunately, most of us remain trapped in our self-created prisons not because of a shortage of opportunities, but because of a deliberate conscious or subconscious intention to focus solely on those beliefs that negate the formation of positive intentions. We have become so engrossed in the day to day activities of life that we forget our true intent in life must be aimed at self-actualization and not merely existing just because we do exist. There is so much more to life than simply existing; existing to pay the bills, existing to mow the lawn or existing to go to work.

There is a definite purpose for everything we do in life, whether that purpose is geared towards the achievement of self-actualization and fulfillment or self-destruction. Most of us are aware of the reasons we partake of the mundane

activities in our daily lives, but are unaware of the true purpose of our lives. We wake up in the morning with the purpose of going to work and we drive home from work with the
purpose of preparing for the next day. But how is it that we
live day by day without a true sense of purpose for our lives?
We perceive our mundane activities as a necessity for our existence, however, consciously or subconsciously place a lesser
value on even a minute change in our belief system that has
the potential to bring about a better life. The reason for this
conclusion is that we do not believe a better life is possible;
therefore we live our lives with the intention of indifference.

The purpose of everything we do in life is decided by us
based on our system of values. For example, our purpose for
waking up in the morning is to go to work to make money.
Obviously, this activity is driven by the value we place on the
production of income and the role it plays. This value gives
purpose to this activity. However, if we can place a significant value on these ancillary activities in order to define their
purpose, we too can place an even greater value on self-actualization and self-fulfillment in order to define a purpose for
our lives.

We may be faced with multiple challenges that may or
may not be a direct result of our actions, for example, the water heater or the iron breaks; the car does not start or we are
greeted with a huge traffic jam, however, we choose to overcome these obstacles in order to fulfill our intended purpose.
Likewise, in life, when we choose a purpose, we too may be
greeted with obstacles that may or may not be a direct result of
our actions, but we must choose to continue to work towards
the ultimate intended purpose. After all, isn't life just a massive collection of smaller purposes? These smaller purposes
all come together to produce a much larger purpose based on
the intentional purpose we choose! We continue to travel to
work in spite of the traffic jam because we perceive that there
will be an immediate repercussion, termination. However, we
dismiss continuing on our path to fulfill our life's chosen purpose because we do not perceive an immediate repercussion.
This is the path of irony chosen by many.

When you decide on a purpose and intent for your life and there is belief and commitment, you grant your life new and improved meaning. No longer do the long drives and traffic jams on the way to work affect you because they do not affect the ultimate purpose you have chosen for your life. They are but a minuscule part of a greater purpose and will not affect the achievement of the intended purpose. The value you place on the attainment of a life of fulfillment will dictate the activities of your life. You must believe in your ability to choose an intended purpose for your life and be fully committed to it in order for you to make it a reality.

What is your purpose in life?

If you are unaware of your purpose, what is prohibiting you from choosing your own purpose?

Notes:

Date:_____

TO CHANGE YOUR LIFE FOR THE BEST INVOLVES THE BEST POSSIBLE CHANGE IN YOUR LIFE

Our life's experiences are a direct and indirect result of our actions. The types of thoughts we foster create our emotional state of mind, which directly and indirectly influences our actions. If we stopped for a second and took the time to analyze the influence our thoughts have on our emotions and actions, we would probably elect to alter these thoughts so that our emotions and consequently our actions too may be altered. Thus, if the results of our actions are directing us away from our goal, it would behoove us to take note of the types of thoughts and the associative emotions that are driving these actions. For example, having empowering thoughts of success and being fully committed to these thoughts will create positive emotions and actions, thus creating positive results. On the other hand, possessing disempowering thoughts and being fully committed to these thoughts, whether consciously or subconsciously, will create negative emotions and actions, thus creating negative results. Likewise, empowering thoughts intertwined with contradicting thoughts of disbelief and fear will also produce negative results.

Every belief, thought and proposed action can be analyzed and compared against the beliefs, thoughts and actions required for the attainment of our goals in order to identify if they are the best possible elections for the expeditious attainment of our goal. If we analyzed our thoughts, decisions and possible actions, we will arrive at a number of different conclusions depending on our level of belief. This exercise will provide a clear indication of the types of beliefs that we typically harbor in our minds.

When we analyze our thoughts and proposed actions in a calm and objective manner, we can decide whether or not these thoughts and actions are productive or detrimental to the attainment of our goals. In principle, any thought or proposed action that is in opposition to our desired goal of abundance and fulfillment signifies the presence of disbelief. However, the process of analyzing our thoughts would probably prove to be a daunting task at best for most, because we literally have thousands of thoughts on a daily basis. However, a sure fire method of identifying our thought type is through the analysis of our emotions and actions, since they are a direct result of the types of thoughts we foster. Additionally, our beliefs can also be identified through the analysis of our thought type.

If you have limiting and fearful thoughts in your mind, you must immediately stop and analyze the potential consequences of these thoughts. How can you arrive at your destination of abundance when your thoughts themselves are limiting? How can you expect to arrive at your destination of abundance when your thoughts are based on fear? We can conclude that the consequences of these types of disempowering thoughts will not aid us in the attainment of our desires but will actually limit us to our current position or potentially to a position that is far worse than our current position.

When we remove the negative and contradictory thoughts and replace them with positive constructive thoughts based on a foundation of true belief, these new and improved empowering thoughts will dictate our actions and therefore create the positive results we desire. In order to obtain the best possible results in our lives, we must constantly monitor our beliefs, thoughts, emotions and actions to verify that they are the best possible election that will produce the most optimal results. When we remain mindful of this, the results of our lives will be astounding.

What potential life changes are you considering?

_____

_____

Are they the best possible changes available?

_____

_____

Notes:

_____

_____

_____

_____

_____

_____

Date:_____

YOUR LIFE STARTS MOVING IN THE RIGHT DIRECTION WHEN YOU MOVE IN THE RIGHT DIRECTION

In order for an object to move in any direction, a force must be applied to it to move it in that particular direction. For example, a ball will not move in any direction until a force, such as a kick, is applied to it to cause it to move in a particular direction. A car will not move in any direction until it is directed by the driver. A plane will not move in a specified direction unless it is directed by the pilot. Likewise, the direction that your life is currently undertaking is based upon the directional force of the path you have chosen.

Your life will not start moving in the right direction unless you too begin to move in the right direction. Your beliefs, thoughts, emotions and your actions are ALL under YOUR control and dictate the directional force of your life. These elements, once correctly directed by you, will cause your life to move in a specific direction based on what you specifically believe. When you truly believe in your ability to achieve success, your thoughts will be those based on your attainment of this success. Your perception plays an important role in this equation and dictates how you view the world around you; all related to what you believe. Your perception dictates what you observe in the "real world". It is through this observation that the answers to your questions or the solutions to your "problems" are found. What you "see", "hear", "taste" and "smell" is based on your belief and perception and as a result you will have specific actions based upon the thoughts that are driven by these beliefs.

The very thoughts that are continually flowing through your mind are based on your current belief system. Therefore, you do have much more control over your life than you may have previously realized. If you desire your life to move in a specific direction, you must first believe that it is possible to move in that specific direction and that you are able to move in that specific direction. Even if you currently believe that your life is in turmoil and that it is impossible to escape its grasp, you still possess the ability to initiate powerful changes in your system of belief. Your current beliefs are never absolutely irrevocable. They are always subject to change and are always changeable by you.

If you were to examine this concept even further, you would find that there are hundreds if not thousands of people who have experienced or are experiencing the exact situation. However, the reason many were able to move beyond the constraints of their perceived dilemma resides in the simple fact that they decided to truly believe that they could and would move beyond their perceived constraints. This shift in their belief system inevitably altered their perception which in turn altered their actions. They began to be more mindful of their actions and subsequently made a continuously conscious effort to locate or create solutions to their "problems". Above all, they were committed to the attainment of their success.

If you mindlessly create the negative situations in your life as opposed to intentionally creating the positive situations in your life, you will continually feel as though you have no control over your life. Ironically the negative situations were originally designed by you in your mind based on your current set of negative beliefs; therefore the manifestations in your life are simply an execution of what you have already decided to believe. The result will inevitably lead to a life of constant complaints about the perceived lack thereof. If you desire your life to move beyond your current situation, you must make a conscious effort to do the same. Complacency, complaining, frustration and fear have no place in the life of someone who is actively seeking fulfillment and abundance. When you focus on eliminating your fears and frustrations, you will be pleasantly surprised at the sheer amount of alternatives that were available to you all along. You must first calm your mind and be willing to look beyond your current perspective and limitations.

Is your life currently moving in the right direction?

Are you moving in the right direction from within?

Notes:

Date:_____

TAKE CONTROL OF YOUR LIFE INSTEAD OF YOUR LIFE TAKING CONTROL OF YOU

Taking control of our lives may seem as though it is an insurmountable task. It may appear as though there are so many things that we have to be concerned about and so little time to get these things accomplished. Often we are frantically running to and fro attempting to get things accomplished in a specific timeframe. However, it seems as though we are always so far behind, never able to catch up. Life itself seems to have a firm grasp on our lives. It seems to control every element and every aspect of our lives to the point where it appears as though we have no other choice but to "go with the flow".

But actually we do have a choice! The question is not whether we have a choice; it is whether we choose to exercise our ability to make powerful choices. We always have multiple choices available to us in each and every situation we incur. Anytime we believe that we have no choice but to "go with the flow", we are allowing our limiting beliefs to control the creation of the experiences in our lives. A life created through the use of limiting beliefs will always be limited. Even if our desires are unlimited, the creation of our lives will always be based on what we believe.

It is my belief that the process of controlling our lives can be subdivided into three separate categories: (a) situational avoidance, (b) situational reaction and (c) situational response.

a) **Situational avoidance**

This is an indication of the proper use of mindfulness as a prelude to everything we do. For example, many of the situations in our lives could have been avoided altogether by careful deliberation of the consequences of our thoughts and actions prior to engagement. Situational avoidance is by far the best alternative.

b) **Situational reaction**

This is an indication of a complete lack of mindfulness, which results in the creation of undesirable situations. A reaction to a situation denotes the presence of fear and frustration. Ironically, the situation automatically becomes worse because our actions are based on the blinding effects of fear and frustration.

c) **Situational response**

This is an indication of the effective use of mindfulness to respond to a directly or indirectly created situation. When we respond to the situation with mindfulness, there is a level of belief and a knowing that there are other alternatives available; we are not relegated to one and only one course of action. Ideally a life based on situational avoidance must be maintained, however during a lapse of mindfulness, situational response is always superior to situational reaction.

In order to control the situation, we must first truly believe that it is possible and the result will be for our greater good. When we truly believe, our thoughts and actions will change to reflect what we believe. We will possess more control over our lives and will make decisions that are indicative of someone who is in control and not out of control. No longer will we allow our decisions to be based on fear and frustration because we know that our decisions can be based on the knowledge that everything will progress for our greater good. Besides, why would we purposely believe that our lives will unfold in a way that is in direct opposition to what we really desire? Unfortunately, this occurs more often than not.

We must intentionally believe that our lives will unfold in a way that creates our ultimate enjoyment and fulfillment. We MUST remain mindful at all times! We must calm our minds and focus on solutions and not the "problem" so that we are always in control and not always out of control. Unfortunately, many of us are too busy focusing on the "problem" and how it affects us emotionally, causing little focus to be allocated towards a solution. Therefore, the "problem" continues to exist while a solution is never found, since it is not within the scope of our focus. When we focus on the solution and not the "problem", we remain in control by not succumbing to the fear based thoughts, actions and frustrations arising from a focus that is solely on the "problem".

Are you controlling your life or is your life controlling you?

How would your life be better if you truly believed in your life of success and fulfillment?

Notes:

Date:_____

BASK IN THE ACCOMPLISHMENTS THAT YOU HAVE ACHIEVED AND OTHERS HAVE NOTICED IN YOU

All too often we do not give ourselves the right amount of credit we deserve. Our friends, family and peers may have convinced us that we should not bask in our accomplishments but should always seek to be modest in the observation of these accomplishments. However, there is no reason we should not be able to celebrate all of our accomplishments. After all, our progress in the realm of mindfulness is what has caused us to acquire these accomplishments in the first place. The fact that you are actively practicing mindfulness on a daily basis, through the constant adjustment of your beliefs and thoughts, so that your actions are specific enough to produce a specific outcome, warrants the expression of accolades from within and without. Therefore, you must by all means bask in your accomplishment, because you have travelled the road less travelled and you have created remarkable changes in your life.

Not only will you notice these changes within yourself, but others will notice them as well. You have allocated your precious time and energy tweaking and re-tweaking your beliefs and thoughts, adding new beliefs and eliminating all of the old unnecessary ones that have strangled your growth. You most certainly deserve it! Do not allow others to dissuade you from the fact that you deserve the accolades that accompany a successful journey through your exercise in mindfulness. Your success and the public display of your appreciation for this success will shine like a beacon of hope to others who are experiencing the same conditions that you once experienced. Therefore, it is your duty to yourself and to others to offer praises of gratitude for a work well done.

*"I tell you the truth, if you have faith
(belief) as small as a mustard seed, you
can say to this mountain, "Move from
here to there" and it will move. Nothing
will be impossible for you."*

Matthew 17:20

"I believe in the power of thought because it is my thought that defines who I am and will become"

- Sidney McCartney

SELF ANALYTICAL QUESTIONNAIRE

Take a moment to answer each of the questions below in the order presented. Think about the implications of your answers and how they have shaped the course of your life up to this point and will continue to shape your life in the future.

- Paint a picture of yourself in your mind. What do you see?
- What is your current emotional state of mind?
- How do you feel about yourself?
- How do you feel about others?
- Do you often feel like a failure?
- Do others view you as a failure?
- What are your saddest childhood memories?
- What are your saddest adulthood memories?
- What are your happiest childhood memories?
- What are your happiest adulthood memories?
- Do you think that your childhood experiences affect your adult experiences?
- Where do you desire to be in life?
- Where do you see yourself heading in life?
- What do you think is limiting you?
- Where would others like for you to be in life?

- Do you think that others are limiting you?
- What are your current beliefs about yourself?
- Where do you think these beliefs about yourself come from?
- Do you think that your beliefs about yourself are valid?
- What beliefs do you have that limit your abilities?
- What do you believe is possible for you to accomplish in your life?
- What do you believe is impossible to accomplish in your life?
- Do you think that you need to change your beliefs about yourself?
- Do you desire to change any beliefs that you have of yourself?
- What can you do to change these beliefs?
- What are your current beliefs about others?
- What beliefs do you think others have of you?
- Where do you think the beliefs that others may have of you stem from?
- Do you think that the beliefs that others have of you are valid?
- Do you think that you should allow the beliefs of others to imprison you?
- Do you think that you need to change the beliefs that others may have of you?
- Do you desire to change any beliefs that you think others have of you?
- What can you do to change the beliefs that others may have of you?
- Which beliefs do you have of yourself that are identical to the beliefs you think others have of you?
- How can you change your beliefs in yourself in order to improve your life?
- How has your past and current beliefs contributed to your current position in life?
- What purpose in life have you chosen?

FORMULAS FOR EMPOWERMENT

EQUATION #1

EQUATION #2

EQUATION #3

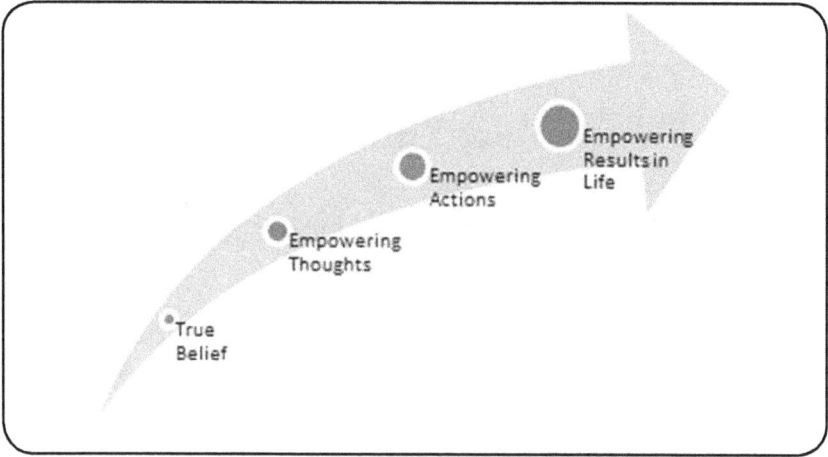

EQUATION #4

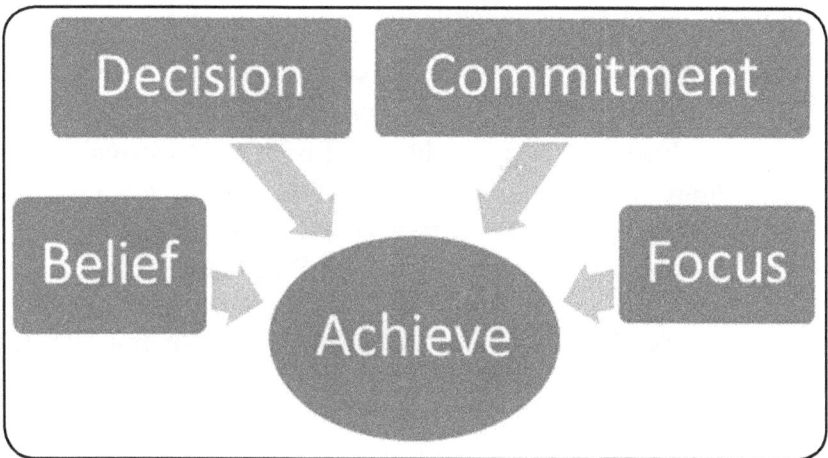

RECAPITULATION PROCESS

1. Where are you currently in life relative to your desires?
2. Which consequences have propelled you to this point?
3. Which actions are creating these consequences?
4. Which emotions are driving these actions?
5. Which thoughts are influencing these emotions?
6. Which beliefs are creating these thoughts?
7. Which core underlying beliefs are producing these beliefs?
8. Access your mental database to uncover the very first memory of these core beliefs.
9. Analyse then dispute the validity of these core beliefs.
10. Intentionally change these core beliefs based on your new beliefs of possibilities (Refer to Appendix IV).
11. Reprogram your mind by continuously focusing on these new core beliefs to eliminate the old habitual beliefs. This can be aided with the use of meditation (Refer to Appendix V).

BELIEF AND POSSIBILITY MATRIX

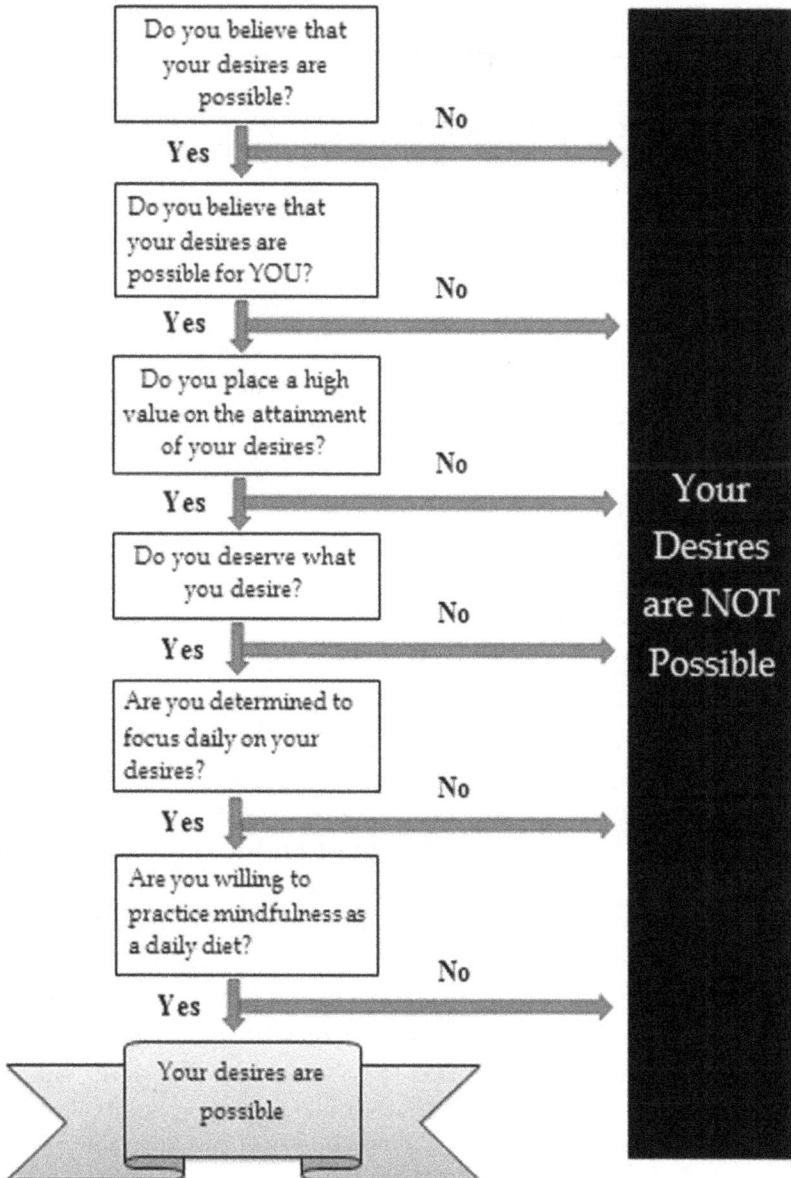

Do you believe that your desires are possible?

No →

Yes ↓

Do you believe that your desires are possible for YOU?

No →

Yes ↓

Do you place a high value on the attainment of your desires?

No →

Yes ↓

Do you deserve what you desire?

No →

Yes ↓

Are you determined to focus daily on your desires?

No →

Yes ↓

Are you willing to practice mindfulness as a daily diet?

No →

Yes ↓

Your desires are possible

Your Desires are NOT Possible

SIMPLE MEDITATION EXERCISE

1. First believe that you will find the answers you seek.
2. Allocate at least 15 minutes for this exercise.
3. Choose a place that is free of distractions.
4. Position yourself comfortably (either sitting or standing).
5. Take the first 5 minutes to focus on your breathing. Take deep breathes by inhaling through your nose and exhaling through your mouth. Focus on your breathing. Do not resist the chaotic thoughts that flow through your mind. Let them flow as you keep your focus fixated on your breathing.
6. Take the next 5 minutes to focus exclusively on a peaceful and tranquil setting in your mind. Resist the urge to wander around the setting. The purpose of this is to train your mind to remain focused. Allow your chaotic thoughts to continue to flow. They will eventually diminish as you continue to focus on your specific setting in your mind. Maintain your breathing.
7. Take the next 5 minutes to focus on your specific intention. Resist the urge to focus on your current "problems" or "dilemmas". The objective here is for you to "see" your life as you desire.

8. Focus on the receipt of an answer to the question that will fill the void between where you currently are and where you desire to be.

INTENTIONAL BELIEF PROCESS

1. Are your desires tangibly possible? (Refer to Appendix IV)
2. Are your desires possible for you? (Refer to Appendix IV)
3. Recapitulate to define which limiting beliefs are limiting you. (Refer to Appendix III)
4. Dispute the validity of these beliefs.
5. Repeat steps 3 and 4 until you are able to answer steps 1 and 2 affirmatively.
6. Replace your original limiting beliefs based on steps 1 and 2 with the new beliefs defined in step 5.
7. Believe in step 1 because others have already attained what you desire.
8. Intentionally believe in step 2 because you value and deserve what is already available for you to receive.

QUESTION & ANSWER

Q: What is hindering my success and why are others able to achieve more than me?

A: Our limiting beliefs are the key elements that are hindering us from achieving our desires. Naturally, this level will vary from person to person based on their experiences, causing some to have more limiting beliefs while others have less. Those who are able to appropriately manage their beliefs by taking steps to identify, dispute and eliminate their limiting beliefs are more prone to success. Some will perform this process almost naturally without much conscious thought, while others will require more intensive measures.

Some individuals are able to inherently modify their old beliefs, thoughts and actions that have been developed and solidified over time because they are consistently mindful of their experiences and how they are affected by what they believe. They essentially are using their experiences to reprogram their core belief system to reflect the necessary changes in order to bring about a different set of experiences. Consequently, in order to move forward, we too must first identify our limiting beliefs and seek to eliminate them by using our undesired experiences as feedback to reprogram our current core belief system. The determining factor depends on our level of commitment.

Q: How do I believe in the face of adversity?

A: Whenever you focus exclusively on the "problem" at hand, that is all you will "see" and your emotions will be adversely affected. Instead, focus exclusively on your enjoyment of a resolution. This will retain your emotions in a heightened state allowing you to believe and think with mindfulness.

Q: What can be done about the things in my life that are out of my control?

A: You have much more direct and indirect control over your life than you realize. However, there will be things that you literally or apparently have no control over. In sitiuation like these, always remember that the outcome of the situation directly depends on how you respond and NOT react to each and every situation, thus allowing you to indeed exercise a level of control over the outcome.

Q: Why do I constantly have disbelief in my mind?

A: The disbelief that lingers in your mind stems from the retention of the old limiting beliefs of the past that are still dictating your present. Identify these limiting beliefs using the recapitulation process (Appendix III) and build awareness of your possibilities using the belief and possibility matrix (Appendix IV).

Q: What do I do when family members are always negative?

A: Beware. It is very easy to adopt our beliefs via association. However, it is always up to us to choose to either accept or refute these beliefs once they are defined as destructive. Through the execution of your positive power potential, your negative family members may perhaps embrace your newly found principles. However, you must realize that each of us is at liberty to choose the direction of our lives. Your negative family members are also at liberty to choose the consequences of their own lives.

Q: Why is my life not heading in the right direction?

A: Your life will head in the exact direction based on your mental vision and focus. This vision is constructed based on what you consciously and subconsciously believe. You must take steps to eliminate your current limiting beliefs (Refer to Appendix III), then through the execution of mindfulness, constantly compare your current beliefs, thoughts and actions to those that are required to attain your goal.

Q: How do I identify my destructive subconscious beliefs?

A: Take a look at your current actions and then identify the thoughts that are driving these actions. Any action based on fear, frustration and limitation reveals the presence of beliefs that are fear, frustration and limitation based. Use the recapitulation process (Appendix III) to identify your "hidden" core beliefs that are creating your conscious and subconscious thoughts.

Q: How do I choose my purpose in life?

A: Your purpose in life is any purpose you so choose. That is the beauty of your ability to choose. There is a vast amount of power potential in each choice you make. Identify your passion in life, choose to execute this passion while not only believing that your passion is possible, but believe that it is possible for YOU (Refer to Appendix IV).

Q: Why does it appear as though I can't seem to get a break in life?

A: How do you "see" your life unfolding in your mind? This vision undoubtedly includes your life being filled with continued issues, "drama" and problems. Your retention of the old past beliefs is creating your life in the present according to how you "see" it in your mind. Eliminate your past beliefs using the recapitulation process (Appendix III) and use the belief and possibility matrix (Appendix IV) to define your possibilities. You must choose to change this destructive vision of what is impossible in your mind so that your life too will change.

Q: How do I manage my thoughts?

A: Managing your thoughts encompasses managing the beliefs that are creating these thoughts. Use the recapitulation process (Appendix III) to define your limiting core beliefs. When you replace these limiting beliefs, the subsequent thoughts that are produced will be reflective of these new beliefs.

Q: Why do I have positive thoughts at times and then negative thoughts at other times?

A: Attempting to maintain positive thoughts without understanding the underlying beliefs that are creating your thoughts will always prove to be futile. The negative thoughts will always resurface because of the presence of negative beliefs. Identify your limiting core beliefs by using the recapitulation process (Appendix III). When you define and replace these beliefs with positive beliefs, your positive thoughts will follow likewise.

Q: How will intentionally believing in what I desire help me to achieve my desires?

A: Belief is a universal force in which we interact with on a daily basis. If you value the outcome of your life, you will desire to retain and focus on only positive beliefs and thoughts. Since your desires have already been accomplished and attained by others, this provides positive proof to you that they are absolutely possible. The remaining belief element is to believe that your desires are possible for YOU. You deserve to have a life of fulfillment and success, so why would you believe and focus on the opposite of this success? Purposely believing in what has already been accomplished by others, knowing that you deserve to receive and will receive your desires, empowers and magnifies your belief intention in your ability to receive what you desire.

Q: Why do I not know what I desire?

A: Even though you may not know exactly what you desire, you know what you do NOT desire. Therefore, what you desire must be the opposite of what you do NOT desire. The limiting beliefs in what is possible are limiting your ability to view possibilities beyond your current scope of belief reality. Refer to the recapitulation process (Appendix III) to identify your limiting beliefs and the belief and possibility matrix (Appendix IV) to define your belief possibilities.

Q: I know what I desire, but can never seem to achieve it?

A: Conflicting imagery is a major misuse of our creative abilities. Often we desire a life of success and fulfillment; however, our beliefs indicate a life filled with continued difficulty. Our mental vision is always constructed based on what we believe, regardless of what we desire. Therefore, a life of desiring success, but believing in opposition to this success will create a mental vision that is contradictory to your desires. Your life will unfold in a manner that will be contradictory to your desires.

Q: Why do I feel nondeserving?

A: Emotions such as nondeservng and not being good enough all stem from the beliefs that we retain from our earliest childhood experiences. Use the recapitulation process (Appendix III) to identify and eliminate these old limiting beliefs.

Q: How specific does my vision of success have to be?

A: The type of car you desire to drive is typically based on specific attributes like colors, price, engine size, type of interior, exterior styling etc. This dictates the type of car you will eventually purchase. Therefore, if you can choose the specifics of the type of car you desire, then how much more so must you identify the specifics in your vision of success that will dictate the type of life you will have.

Q: How can I achieve success?

A: Success is achieved through mindfully deliberating your current beliefs and thoughts to ensure that they are driving your actions in the correct direction. Define the beliefs, thoughts and actions that are required to achieve your goals. Compare them with your current beliefs, thoughts and actions. Through the use of mindfulness, you will be able to promote awareness of the deficiencies between your current actions and the actions required to achieve your goals. Your emotions will provide you with the needed feedback to identify when the consequences are contrary to your desires. Remember, instant gratification only temporarily masks the symptoms and does not solve anything.

Q: How do I obtain the strength necessary to maintain my commitment to my goal?

A: You are always creating your life even when you choose to do nothing to promote your life of success. The commitment to your goal will depend on the value attached to the attainment of this goal. If you value your life of success, why would you create anything but success? You have the power to create a life that is VOID of success and therefore you have the power to create a life that is full of success. Keep your focus constantly fixated on your life of success and avoid harboring beliefs and thoughts that are in opposition to this success.

Q: What do I do when I feel as though I have no control over a situation?

A: Your feeling of being out of control is always based on disbelief in the possibility and ability to achieve your desires. Even when you feel like your life is out of control, you are still in control of your life because your life is actually being created via the conflicting imagery of your beliefs. Use the recapitulation process (Appendix III) to identify and eliminate the limiting core beliefs that are creating resistance in your life. So instead of creating a life based on old past limiting beliefs, you can recreate your life based on your new belief of possibilities.

Q: How do I eliminate my limiting thoughts of disbelief?

A: The recapitulation process (Refer to Appendix III) identifies your old limiting beliefs, while the belief and possibility matrix (Refer to Appendix IV) can be used to expand your view of what is possible in your life.

Q: How do I believe that what is literally possible is actually possible for me?

A: We believe in the air that flows all around us because this belief is solidified through our continuous interaction with it even though we are not able to physically see it. This air is an "unseen" force that has the ability to sustain life and also to take life depending on how it is used. Believing is no different. When something is literally possible, especially when it has already been accomplished by others, this indicates that the receipt of this possibility is up for the taking. However, our limiting beliefs always block the receipt of these desires into our lives. Ironically, if we can choose to believe in the impossibilities of things that are obviously possible, we too can choose to believe in the receipt of things that are obviously possible. When we intentionally choose to believe, our vision of success is built on this vision. As we continuously focus on this vision, our belief is solidified through our continuous interaction with this vision. Therefore, just like the air around us that we cannot see but choose to believe in its ability to keep us alive, so too will we believe in the possibility of our life of success.

www.ingramcontent.com/pod-product-compliance
Lightning Source LLC
Chambersburg PA
CBHW051747040426
42446CB00007B/249